Life

EVERYONE HAS A STORY

Marilyn ~
I hope this book
blesses you!
Dianne Tolliver

Life

EVERYONE HAS A STORY

DIANNE TOLLIVER

XULON PRESS

Xulon Press
2301 Lucien Way #415
Maitland, FL 32751
407.339.4217
www.xulonpress.com

Unless otherwise indicated, Scripture quotations taken from the Holy Bible, New International Version (NIV). Copyright © 1973, 1978, 1984, 2011 by Biblica, Inc.™. Used by permission. All rights reserved.

Scripture quotations taken from the King James Version (KJV)–*public domain.*

Printed in the United States of America.

ISBN-13: 978-1-6305-0166-2

Dedication

To Brooke, Mark, and Michele —
Thank you for your love, support,
and encouragement.

To the remarkable people who courageously
shared their personal and inspirational stories
to make this book a reality.

A Special Note
of Appreciation and Thanks

*The following people provided invaluable
support during this book journey. Thank you!*

Barbara Butler
Bunni Cooper
Jonny Coleman
Bev Hayes
Barbara Heard

Contents

Introduction

Have you ever stopped to ask yourself, "What am I doing with my life? Where am I going? What should I do next?"

Soon after completing the book, *Living Through Troubled Times — Witnessing the Rainbow*, I was confused about the next steps God wanted me to embrace. As I prayed and asked for guidance, it was quiet. I found myself wandering into uncharted territory, not knowing where I should focus my time and energy. Should I write a sequel to the book or perhaps return to full-time leadership consulting? Did God have a completely different plan for me? My thoughts bounced from one thing to another. No matter how many times I prayed and asked for direction, there was silence.

The uncertainty made me very anxious and uncomfortable. In the past, I prayed, set goals, established a plan with a corresponding schedule, then invested the time and effort required to achieve the desired results. This approach always yielded successful outcomes and made me feel safe. But this time, my situation was very different. I was stuck and unclear as to what God wanted me to do next.

Then, one summer day after church, a dear friend looked straight in my eyes and said, "Perhaps living with the unknown, resting, and waiting on the Lord is what you should be doing right now." With that "ah-ha" moment, I went home and embraced two Bible verses, as I waited for direction and guidance from God.

*"Wait for the Lord; be strong and take heart
and wait for the Lord." Psalm 27:14 (NIV)*

"...those who hope in the Lord will renew their strength.
They will soar on wings like eagles;
they will run and not grow weary;
they will walk and not be faint."
Isaiah 40:31 (NIV)

Finally, just before Thanksgiving, I awoke with a clear focus. God answered my prayers. A sequel to the book was my next journey! With new clarity, I thanked God and began to outline the chapter titles and the people I should interview. However, the thought of conducting heart-wrenching interviews and writing another book exhausted me. So, I hit the "pause button" and "placed my hope in the Lord to renew my strength," so I could write once again.

In early March the following year, I realized my mind, heart, and energy aligned with God's next steps for me. It was as if a light switch turned on. I was inspired and excited to write once again. And so, stepping out in faith, I pulled out my notes from four months earlier and began this book journey.

The resulting true stories, captured in the pages ahead, share the unplanned journeys of my friends, family, and acquaintances. The stories provide an unfiltered glimpse into their joys, challenges, and heartbreaks while revealing God's love, compassion, and strength. Due to sensitive topics and privacy protection, some names were changed in the stories. Each chapter concludes with thought-provoking questions to provide you with a time of personal reflection.

I hope you are encouraged and blessed by the stories encapsulated in this book. Life is not always easy, but remember — you are never alone. God is with you! God is with us on our journey.

Blessings, Dianne

Releasing Your Fears to God

"So do not fear, for I am with you; do not be dismayed,
for I am your God. I will strengthen you and help you;
I will uphold you with my righteous right hand."
Isaiah 41:10 (NIV)

The doctor was short and to the point, "Dianne, we have the results of your CAT Scan. Unfortunately, there is a mass in your brain. You have an appointment with the head of neurosurgery at UCLA tomorrow at 10 AM. I'm sorry." Shocked and stunned, she just sat there. There were no words to express the overwhelming fear that filled her body.

At age thirty-one, Dianne was living life to the fullest. She was the proud mother of a beautiful, two-month-old son, and had recently celebrated her ninth wedding anniversary. She was leading a successful organization for an information technology company and was actively involved with her church. Simply put, her life was amazing.

However, as the weeks passed, Dianne began to experience dizzy spells that significantly impacted her ability to concentrate and function. She went to the doctor, and he attributed her symptoms to stress. Dianne thought his diagnosis was probably correct. She felt extremely guilty for working outside the home and leaving her son, even though her loving parents were taking great care of him. She also went to a chiropractor, in an attempt to alleviate her intolerable spinning, but nothing seemed to make a difference. Her dizziness only intensified.

Then one evening, while cooking dinner, she reached for a glass bowl in her kitchen cabinet, but she was unable to maintain her grasp. The bowl came crashing down on the countertop, and glass flew everywhere. Fortunately, her baby was in the other room and safe, but at that moment, a tinge of fear flew through her body. She realized something was wrong. It felt as if her brain was sending signals to her hand, but her hand was not functioning correctly. She didn't say anything, but deep down realized her dizziness and hand issues might be connected.

The following week, on a Thursday morning, Dianne was quietly sitting at her office desk. After looking through some papers, she attempted to sign a document, but her signature came out backward. Dianne panicked and immediately called her doctor's office. Fortunately, the nurse was able to squeeze her in for an appointment that same morning. After a short examination, the doctor ordered a brain CAT scan. Dianne notified her husband and parents, and they began to pray.

> *"Then you will call on me and come and pray to me,*
> *and I will listen to you." Jeremiah 29:12 (NIV)*

After the scan, Dianne stopped by her parent's house to have lunch and kiss her son. Despite her dizziness, she returned to work, while her son took his afternoon nap. She wanted to keep her mind busy, as she impatiently waited for the doctor to call with the scan results.

Within a few hours, her office phone rang. As Dianne picked up the phone, she heard the voice of her doctor's nurse, but something was not right. The nurse's voice was trembling as she said, "We have the results from your CAT Scan. We need you to meet with the doctor this afternoon. Please bring your husband." Dianne asked if everything was okay, but the nurse just repeated her original statement.

As she slowly hung up the phone, Dianne sensed the news regarding her scan was not good. She immediately contacted her husband and family — they continued to pray. That afternoon, the doctor relayed the devastating diagnosis, "There is a mass in your brain. You have an appointment with the head of neurosurgery at UCLA tomorrow at 10 AM. I'm sorry."

Dianne was devastated, and unable to speak, as she attempted to process the shocking diagnosis. Her husband took the lead to gather the required information for the appointment the next morning, then thanked the doctor. He was privately informed that the situation did not look good, but he protected his wife from this gut-wrenching news.

That evening, the family gathered at Dianne's home as members of her church began to pray. They realized her situation desperately needed God's healing hands. Their pastor was out of town at a minister's retreat, but he called their home when he heard the news. He decided to meet them on the UCLA campus the next morning, and join them for the appointment with the neurosurgeon. At his request, the pastors at the retreat prayed for Dianne's complete healing.

After a restless night, Dianne awoke early to spend time with her baby. As she lovingly rocked little Scott in their lazy-boy rocker, the gravity of her situation began to sink in. She may never see Scott take his first steps, attend his first day in kindergarten, ride a bike, or graduate from high school. The enormity of the situation was overwhelming and difficult to grasp. She tried to pray for herself, but the words would not come.

As Dianne walked into her son's nursery, she slowly packed some of his clothes, taking time to admire some of her favorite little outfits. Since the UCLA hospital was about 150 miles from their home, they decided it was best if Scott spent the day with her parents. Then, without much thought, she packed an overnight bag for herself, in case they needed to spend the night at the hospital.

Just before dawn, they put Scott in the car and headed for her parent's home, about five minutes away. Dianne tried to hold back tears as she kissed her son goodbye and carefully handed him to her mother. As tears rolled down her mother's face, her father sobbed. Dianne hugged them goodbye, then gave Scott one more kiss on his forehead before getting into the car.

It was gut-wrenching as her husband began to back the car out of the driveway. Dianne quietly watched her parents helplessly standing on the front porch, waving goodbye, and lovingly holding her son. They were trying to be brave. Then Dianne thought, "What if I don't survive?" She knew the entire situation was now in God's hands.

"The Lord is good to those whose hope is in him,
to the one who seeks him." Lamentations 3:25 (NIV)

The drive across the desert, through the San Fernando Valley, then finally to the UCLA campus, seemed to take an eternity. Dianne and her husband exchanged only a few words during the long drive; it was just too emotional to talk. Upon arriving at the large UCLA hospital, they found a parking space, then commenced the search for the right building and office.

Then, a remarkable and comforting thing happened. As Dianne and her husband looked across the campus, their pastor was coming up the walkway. They were shocked to "just run into him." This simple gift immediately gave both of them a sense of God's peace. They knew they were not on this journey alone. God was with them.

"...For the Lord comforts his people and will have
compassion on his afflicted ones." Isaiah 49:13 (NIV)

After a two-hour wait, the nurse called Dianne's name. As she nervously made her way into the examination room with her husband, their pastor remained in the waiting room and quietly prayed. A few minutes later, the doctor entered the exam room. After a brief review of her symptoms, he carefully reviewed the CAT Scan results, moving from one view to another. He then had Dianne perform a variety of simple balancing movements. It was difficult due to her dizziness, but she concentrated extremely hard. She wanted to pass all the tests.

After a few moments of silence, the doctor said he needed to conduct a Magnetic Resonance Imaging (MRI) brain scan, but it would take four to six weeks to get an appointment since the technology was still relatively new, and they only had one machine (the year was 1989). The doctor then excused himself to check on the schedule.

A few moments later, the doctor walked back into the room with a perplexed look on his face and shared, "You are not going to believe this. We just had a cancellation. We can conduct your MRI scan in one hour. I will review the results on Saturday morning, then meet with you after my morning rounds at the hospital." The doctor was surprised there was a last-minute appointment available, but Dianne and her husband knew this was not a coincidence. God was in control of the situation, and they were once again comforted.

> *"Peace I leave with you; my peace I give you.*
> *I do not give to you as the world gives. Do not let your hearts*
> *be troubled and do not be afraid." John 14:27 (NIV)*

Within an hour, Dianne found herself inside the dark, narrow tube of the MRI scanner. She was strapped down and unable to move. The top of the machine was one inch from her nose. Unable to focus her eyes, claustrophobia began to set in. As she thought about her situation and this mass in her brain, her heart began to race as her eyes filled with tears.

It was at this point, broken and afraid, Dianne turned all of her energy and focus toward God, and she whispered, "God, help me." Then, she prayed and asked God to remove the mass in her head.

> *"But when you ask, you must believe and not doubt,*
> *because the one who doubts is like a wave of the sea,*
> *blown and tossed by the wind." James 1:6 (NIV)*

Instantly, all of Dianne's anxiety and fears left her body. She could feel God's peace and love surrounding her inside the cold, dark tube. As she began to praise Him, a remarkable phenomenon occurred. A powerful, quivering energy began to reverberate at the bottom of her feet. This energy then intensified as it traveled up her legs, through her torso, past her heart, to her brain, then it left through the top of her head. It was unlike anything she had ever experienced in her lifetime.

As the vibrating energy left her body, she was filled with an indescribable sense of peace. She knew at that moment; God healed her. She was no longer afraid.

> *"Ah, Sovereign Lord, you have made the heavens and the earth*
> *by your great power and outstretched arm.*
> *Nothing is too hard for you." Jeremiah 32:17 (NIV)*

The entire situation took her breath away, and she immediately shared her experience with her husband and pastor. She was at peace and enjoyed a relaxing lunch and dinner. That night, they stayed in a local hotel, and she had no problems with dizziness. In her heart, she knew God was in control.

On Saturday morning, they went back to the hospital and waited for over two hours for the doctor to finish his morning rounds. Finally, as Dianne looked down the long hallway, she saw her doctor walking toward her. She jumped out of her chair and ran toward him. The doctor smiled, held out his arms, and said, "You're okay. There is no mass. You have a hole in your brain that we cannot explain. I want you to come back in six months for a follow-up MRI scan as a precautionary measure, but everything looks good." With tears in her eyes, Dianne hugged the doctor and quietly thanked God for healing her. That evening they returned home and praised God with their family.

> *"He is the one you praise; he is your God, who*
> *performed for you those great and awesome wonders*
> *you saw with your own eyes." Deuteronomy 10:21 (NIV)*

The following morning, Dianne stood in front of her church congregation to thank them for their prayers, and publicly praise God for healing her. Her dizziness and other symptoms went away, with no additional treatments required. Six months later, she returned to UCLA for a follow-up MRI scan. After a careful review, the doctor said, "Go enjoy a great life! I do not need to see you again."

> *"Praise the Lord. Praise God in his sanctuary;*
> *Praise him in his mighty heavens.*
> *Praise him for his acts of power;*
> *Praise him for his surpassing greatness."*
> *Psalm 150:1-2 (NIV)*

In closing, Dianne shared, "I will never forget the way my Heavenly Father lovingly took care of me. Thirty years later, I still have a hole in my brain and view it as a constant reminder of God's power. I will forever be grateful. Praise be to God!"

"But as for me, I watch in hope for the Lord;
I wait for God my Savior; my God will hear me."
Micah 7:7 (NIV)

Dianne and Scott

REFLECTION

Take a moment to answer the questions below. You can write your thoughts in this book or use a separate journal.

God yearns for us to live in peace, but sometimes our human minds and hearts become fearful. At one point, Dianne was unable to pray for herself due to her overwhelming fear of the situation she was facing.

1. Pause and Reflect. Do you recall a time in your life when fear over-whelmed you? If yes, what happened? What did you do? Were you able to pray and ask God to help you?

_____

_____

_____

_____

_____

_____

2. Have you been in a situation where God comforted you or provided a clear direction? If yes, what happened?

_____

_____

_____

_____

_____

_____

NEXT STEPS

1. When Dianne was afraid and unable to pray for herself, she asked her family and church congregation to pray for her. In the space below, write the names of three people who will pray for you, no matter what situation you are facing:

    _____

    _____

    _____

    _____

    _____

2. *"Let everything that has breath praise the Lord..."* Psalm 150:6 (NIV)
    Take a moment and thank God for the blessings in your life.

    _____

    _____

    _____

    _____

CLOSING PRAYER

Dear Heavenly Father,

At times I have been paralyzed by fear due to situations and events in my life. Please help me to remember that you are always with me, regardless of my problems or circumstances. At all times, you know what I am thinking and how I feel, even when I am unable to find the words to pray.

Thank you for carrying me through my emotional, physical, and mentally tough times. Thank you for your unconditional love. You are an awesome God! Amen.

Unexpected Blessings

"Heal me, Lord, and I will be healed;
save me, and I will be saved,
for you are the one I praise." Jeremiah 17:14 (NIV)

Franklin suddenly sat down — something didn't feel right. As he dropped his head and covered his face with his hands, he vaguely heard his trainer saying, "Franklin, are you alright? Are you okay? Do we need to call an ambulance?" After a few moments passed, Franklin slowly lifted his head to respond, but no words came out of his mouth — he was unable to speak. As fear rushed through his body, he began to grasp that something was drastically wrong.

At age fifty-two, Franklin was balancing a full life as a vibrant pastor, loving father, and devoted husband. Week after week, he delivered inspiring sermons to help people meet God for the first time, and help others deepen their spiritual journey here on earth. He enjoyed connecting with people from all nationalities and backgrounds, whether young or old, rich or poor. Franklin loved the gift of talking and interacting with others to spread the good news about Jesus.

Then, one cold winter day in Northern Virginia, Franklin's life changed in a matter of seconds. It was his standard "telework day," but on this particular Friday, he felt compelled to meet his trainer at the gym instead of remaining home alone. This last-minute change to his Friday routine may have saved his life. It is the first of several instances where God's presence is apparent in Franklin's story.

The gym was about forty minutes away and close to the church where Franklin pastored. So, he got in his old car and safely drove through heavy traffic before reaching the fitness center. Upon his arrival, he felt great and was ready for a good workout. After saying hello to his trainer, he started his usual warm-up routine, which consisted of jumping rope 125 times. As Franklin counted the number of times he jumped, something seemed to change in his brain when he reached "twenty-five." There was no pain, just a change in how he felt. It was odd.

He immediately sat down and put his head in the palms of his hands. When he glanced up, his trainer said, "Franklin, are you alright?" When he tried to respond, no words came out of his mouth — he was unable to speak. From that point forward, everything seemed to transition to slow motion. It sounded as if the people around him were talking in an echo chamber. In his mind and through his confusion, he started talking with God, "Lord, what is going on? I'm young. I don't understand this."

"Then you will call on me
and come and pray to me,
and I will listen to you." Jeremiah 29:12 (NIV)

Franklin recalls hearing, "Do we need to call an ambulance?" As he shook his head "no," his trainer laid him on the floor, and the gym manager dialed 911. While they waited for the ambulance and firefighters to arrive, Franklin was able to move his arms and legs. Then, the ability to make sounds came back, but he was still unable to formulate any words. Cognitively, he knew what he wanted to say, but he could not speak.

By this time, the trainer was able to reach Franklin's wife, Val, by dialing the emergency contact on his phone. He quickly explained the situation, but she was confused. She thought he was working from home. When Val hung up the phone, a sudden peace from God fell over her. She knew her husband would be okay. This peace remained with her through Franklin's hospital stay and throughout his recuperation journey.

"And the peace of God,
which transcends all understanding,

Life Everyone Has a Story

will guard your hearts and your minds in Christ Jesus."
Philippians 4:7 (NIV)

When the ambulance technicians arrived, they took Franklin's vitals and asked him some basic questions, "What is your name? Where do you work? What's your wife's name?" He knew all the answers but was unable to respond and felt trapped in his own body. As the hectic situation unfolded around him, Franklin continued his conversation with God, "Lord, this is your voice, if you decide I can't have it, I'm fine. It is yours."

"Therefore, I urge you, brothers and sisters,
in view of God's mercy, to offer your bodies
as a living sacrifice, holy and pleasing to God —
this is your true and proper worship." Romans 12:1 (NIV)

As the emergency technicians loaded Franklin into the ambulance, they continued to ask him questions. His vital signs were stable, and he was moving his face, arms, and legs — all good signs. Then, as the technicians conversed with the hospital, Franklin heard the words, "Priority. Priority." Suddenly, the ambulance sirens switched on as the driver pressed down on the gas pedal. A full emergency team was waiting for Franklin when the ambulance arrived.

The emergency room was chaotic as the specialists tried to determine what was wrong with Franklin. He did not show many of the typical signs of a stroke, so they were perplexed. However, time was of the essence to administer a shot to reverse his symptoms — if it was indeed a stroke. If they made the wrong call, Franklin could "bleed out," but there was no time to run additional tests.

"Have mercy on me, Lord, for I am faint;
heal me, Lord..." Psalm 6:2 (NIV)

Finally, the lead doctor said, "GO with the shot." A few minutes later, Franklin's ability to formulate words began to return. He was grateful and praised the Lord. He knew it was not a coincidence that he had a top-notch doctor. God placed Franklin five minutes from one of the best hospitals in America due to his unplanned workout session.

As Franklin laid in the emergency room, hooked up to a variety of machines, an emotional situation unfolded. He shared, "I saw a young woman who just lost her baby as the result of a miscarriage. She was wailing with grief and did not have a family member with her. As a doctor spoke to the woman, he was translating the situation to someone on her cell phone. She continued to sob, and my heart broke for her. I wanted to help her but realized I was unable to get up due to my predicament, so I prayed for her as I laid on my gurney. Her situation left a lasting impression in my heart."

As Franklin's ability to speak continued to return, he started joking with the hospital staff. Deep down, he feared he would cry if he didn't keep his mind preoccupied as the doctors ran test after test. They needed to ensure there were no blood clots or other risk factors that required immediate attention. As Franklin continued to lay in the emergency room, vulnerable and full of fear, his cell phone unexpectedly rang.

"There is no fear in love.
But perfect love drives out fear..."
1 John 4:18 (NIV)

When Franklin said hello, he heard the voice of an older man from his church — a man who survived a severe stroke several years earlier. This man had limited speaking abilities, but on this day and at this time, he spoke clearly and precisely. His words encouraged Franklin's heart. At that moment, God spoke to Franklin, and he heard these exact words in his head, "The reason he is calling you — is so that you will know — you will be alright." God provided an unexpected "glimpse of grace" in the middle of his fear.

"...For the Lord comforts his people
and will have compassion on his afflicted ones."
Isaiah 49:13 (NIV)

Soon after the call, Val arrived at the hospital. Her presence calmed Franklin. She shared the overwhelming sense of peace God gave her regarding his situation. Her words comforted him. It was clear that God was working through others to provide peace and hope.

"Every good and perfect gift is from above..."
James 1:17 (NIV)

For the next four days, Franklin remained in the intensive care unit of the hospital as his doctors ran a wide variety of tests. Through an MRI scan, the doctors confirmed he had a stroke. As time passed, Franklin began to experience other "classic stroke symptoms," including numbness in his face, arm, and leg. However, some of the symptoms were not tracking with the location of his stroke, so doctors ordered additional tests.

Despite the numerous tests, his doctors were perplexed and unable to explain some of his symptoms. When they were comfortable that Franklin was out of danger, he was moved out of the intensive care unit, then released from the hospital the following day. Throughout the entire ordeal, Franklin continued to trust God as he tried his best to surrender his fear and anxiety to Him. Val's continued peace regarding his stroke was a great comfort to both of them and another affirmation that God was in control of the situation.

Two weeks after his stroke, Franklin stood up in front of the church congregation and preached a full sermon, grateful for every word that left his mouth. As he began to speak, he shared his gratitude for the miracles he witnessed over the past few weeks, and the blessings he received from God through his family and friends.

"You intended to harm me,
but God intended it for good to accomplish
what is now being done, the saving of many lives."
Genesis 50:20 (NIV)

As a result of his stroke, Franklin has a renewed sense of gratitude and appreciation for the power of God's blessings. He shared, "In the past, I felt uncomfortable accepting help from others, but when I was flat on my back and unable to speak, there was nothing I could do. As a direct result of my stroke, I experienced the way God engages people to intervene, support, and help others in times of need. Blessings from God are a powerful gift that I am learning to accept."

"And my God will meet all your needs
according to the riches of his glory in Christ Jesus."
Philippians 4:19 (NIV)

He went on to share, "God is at work through His people. Giving and accepting is part of God's plan. Take time to notice the blessings in your life and be grateful."

"And God is able to bless you abundantly, so that in
all things at all times, having all that you need,
you will abound in every good work."
2 Corinthians 9:8 (NIV)

Several months have passed since Franklin lost his ability to speak due to his stroke. Through some minor setbacks, he is learning the importance of rest without feeling guilty or uncomfortable. After all, God emphasizes the importance of rest.

"For in six days the Lord made the heavens
and the earth, the sea, and all that is in them,
but he rested on the seventh day."
Exodus 20:11 (NIV)

Franklin shared, "There is no way of knowing if another stroke will be part of my future. When fear creeps into my mind about the unknown, I turn my anxiety over to my Heavenly Father and ask Him for strength and peace to move forward. As I fully trust God with my life, He continues to shine a light on my next steps, one day at a time. In life, there will be good times, and there will be trials, but through it all, God is with us.

"In all your ways submit to him,
and he will make your paths straight."
Proverbs 3:6 (NIV)

In closing, he shared, "We are only here for a short amount of time, and I plan to make the most of my time. I am grateful for my blessings and the opportunity to serve a loving Father. Praise be to God."

REFLECTION

Within a split second, Franklin's life unexpectedly changed.

1. Has someone close to you experienced a life-altering event? If you answered yes, in what ways did God provide strength, peace, and support during and after the incident?

_____

_____

_____

_____

_____

2. Take a moment and write down the blessings in your life and the things you sometimes take for granted. Pause and thank God!

_____

_____

_____

_____

_____

_____

_____

_____

_____

NEXT STEPS

If today was your last day on earth, what would you say to the people in your life? Jot down your thoughts below and pray over your list. Then, if you are comfortable, share your thoughts and feelings through a personal visit, phone call, text, letter, or card. It's not too late! Be proactive!

_____

_____

_____

_____

_____

_____

_____

_____

_____

CLOSING PRAYER

Dear Heavenly Father,

Thank you for being with me every moment of every day. Thank you for the good times and my many blessings. Thank you for providing me with peace, strength, and wisdom during the tough times of my life. I love you. Amen.

The Gift of Friendship

"For I know the plans I have for you," declares the Lord,
"plans to prosper you and not to harm you,
plans to give you hope and a future."
Jeremiah 29:11 (NIV)

Bunni's fiancé had errands to run before they met for a late dinner, so she decided to leave the office and drive home. As she maneuvered through traffic, an unsettled feeling rushed through her body. She suddenly felt compelled to take a detour and drive by the apartment of a woman who previously pursued her fiancé. As Bunni drove down the street where the woman lived, she saw her fiancé's truck. Her heart began to pound as God gave her the courage to get out of the car and knock on the woman's door.

Bunni and her younger sister grew up in a conservative home in Northern Virginia. Their father was a pastor, and their mother was actively involved in the church as a pastor's wife. They were terrific parents but were very protective. They established strict rules regarding who their daughters were allowed to date. The girls "grew up" with the boys in their church youth group, and looked forward to meeting men on their own. They dreamed of going to college, falling in love, and getting married before they were twenty-two. After all, it was the sixties, and women married young.

"Many are the plans in a person's heart,
but it is the Lord's purpose that prevails."
Proverbs 19:21 (NIV)

Before long, Bunni moved to a different state to attend a Christian college. Making new friends was easy for her. She had an outgoing, bubbly personality, and genuinely cared about people. She had several "guy" friends, but there was no one special in her life. During Bunni's junior year, she dated a young man who was studying to be a pastor, but there was no "spark," so they decided to part ways.

The summer before Bunni's senior year, she prayed, "God, I don't know what I'm looking for in a husband or what the future holds, but can you please allow me to have a date for all the special college events during my senior year? I don't want to go alone." As Bunni's senior year progressed, she was grateful to attend every special event with a date. God was faithful and blessed her.

Bunni finished her senior year without a special man in her life, but she enjoyed a large circle of friends, comprised of both men and women. At the time, she had no idea this group of people would bless her for a lifetime. One day, her mother jokingly said, "Bunni, the reason you don't have a boyfriend is because you treat all the men in your life like brothers." Bunni paused and thought, "Perhaps my mother's right, but if the men in my life view me as a sister — that's okay with me. I want to be a friend that people can count on at all times. I am truly blessed."

"A friend loves at all times,
and a brother is born for a time of adversity."
Proverbs 17:17 (NIV)

After graduation, Bunni moved back home and settled into a new job. Even though she dated regularly, she soon inherited the label "single woman." This label made her feel uncomfortable, so she decided to break the stereotype. Bunni chose to skip the "singles" group at church, and instead volunteered to teach the "Kindergarten Sunday School" class. She loved being around children and looked forward to becoming a mother someday.

Despite Bunni's strong faith in God, she felt unsettled as her friends married and had children. So, she made a conscious decision to enlarge her social group to include married couples and no longer worry about "being the fifth wheel." Then, an unexpected thing happened. As the young couples began to have children, Bunni decided to "unofficially adopt" their kids as her nieces and nephews. She soon embraced the name "Auntie Bun-Bun." God blessed her as she found love, joy, and happiness through others.

"My command is this:
Love each other as I have loved you."
John 15:12 (NIV)

During her mid-twenties, she dated one man for over two years. Her parents and friends loved him, and Bunni thought, "he might be the one." Then, one day, he said he was going camping with friends for a week and would call when he returned home. She loved him and looked forward to his return. When the week passed, he never called. She tried many times to reach him, but he walked out of her life without an explanation. They never spoke again. Bunni's heart broke as her trust in men shattered. Thankfully, during this gut-wrenching time of her life, God provided comfort through her friends, church family, and His promises in the Bible.

"Cast all your anxiety on him
because he cares for you." 1 Peter 5:7 (NIV)

After a great deal of soul searching, Bunni dusted herself off and re-entered the dating world. During this time, she continued to expand her friendships and gather additional "adopted" nieces and nephews. In her late twenties, she met a man at work, and they began to date. They quickly fell in love and were engaged.

Bunni loved him with her whole heart, but soon discovered he was involved with other women while on business travel. She was devastated and broke-off their engagement. After six months passed, he begged for a second chance. Bunni once again opened her heart, and they resumed their engagement. Despite their engagement, she prayed, "Lord, please give me the courage to leave him, if he ever cheats again."

"Finally, be strong in the Lord
and in His mighty power." Ephesians 6:10 (NIV)

Then one day, Bunni's fiancé "had errands to run" before they met for a late dinner, so she decided to leave the office and drive home. As she worked her way through traffic, an unsettled feeling rushed through her body — a feeling she later attributed to the Lord. She suddenly felt compelled to take a detour and drive by the apartment of a young woman who previously pursued her fiancé.

As Bunni drove down the street where the woman lived, she saw her fiancé's truck. Her heart began to pound as God gave her the courage to get out of the car and knock on the woman's door. The events that unfolded over the next few moments were gut-wrenching. Her finance was having an affair. Bunni was devastated, but God intervened and gave her the courage to walk away from the engagement and their three-year relationship.

"Whoever walks in integrity walks securely,
but whoever takes crooked paths will be found out."
Proverbs 10:9 (NIV)

Bunni was a private person, so she only told a few friends about the affair but never discussed the situation with her family. She spared people the unpleasant details, and simply said, "our relationship didn't work out." Bunni was heartbroken, humiliated, and emotionally exhausted, so she once again took a break from dating. As she looked up to God for guidance and direction, her friends surrounded her with love and compassion.

"Be strong and courageous. Do not be afraid or
terrified because of them, for the Lord your God goes with you;
he will never leave you nor forsake you." Deuteronomy 31:6 (NIV)

When Bunni turned thirty-six, she realized her biological clock was ticking, and motherhood might not be part of her future. Before long, she began to date a wonderful friend from the office, and their relationship grew into love. He treated her with respect and kindness. Then one day, after dating for two years, she noticed he was quiet at dinner and asked if he was okay. He responded, "I have something to tell you." Bunni's stomach immediately tied into knots as she braced herself. He shared, "I met another woman, and I want to date her."

Bunni's heart broke once again. She fell into a period of grief and despair. She shared, "I felt defeated. I didn't know if I had the energy to pursue future relationships and possibly face another disappointment. I'm grateful for my friends and family who once again carried me through this painful time, and for my Heavenly Father who sustained me." Bunni sadly faced the reality that motherhood would not be a part of her life, but was grateful for her "adopted" nieces and nephews.

> *"Trust in the Lord with all your heart and lean not*
> *on your own understanding; in all your ways*
> *submit to him, and he will make your paths straight."*
> *Proverbs 3:5-6 (NIV)*

In her forties, Bunni dabbled with online dating but became disheartened with this approach. She also contemplated adoption but never followed through. As she entered her fifties, her mother's health began to decline, so they decided to share a home. They enjoyed several years together until her mother passed away at the age of ninety-one. Bunni was devastated. Thankfully, God once again provided comfort through her family and circle of friends.

She shared, "My friends were such a comfort when I lost my Mom. They compassionately listened, cried with me, provided meals, and carried me through my grief. I will forever be grateful for the wonderful friends God has lovingly provided throughout my life."

Bunni is now in her seventies and enjoys an active social life. She said, "My life is full of blessings, and I am happy. My journey here on earth is different than my original dream, but I'm grateful for my family and friends across the country. I now have over two-hundred "adopted" nieces and nephews. My friends include me in their children's baptisms, graduations, weddings, and other special events — it warms my heart."

> *"And we know that in all things God works*
> *for the good of those who love him, who have*
> *been called according to his purpose."*
> *Romans 8:28 (NIV)*

Bunni continued, "While I never had children of my own, God blessed me with the honor of loving and praying for many wonderful toddlers, youngsters, and teenagers. Several of my "adopted" nieces and nephews are now adults, so I am a Great Aunt to a new generation of kids. I am also honored to work with special needs children at an elementary school — they touch my heart every day."

> *"May the God of hope fill you with all joy and peace*
> *as you trust in him, so that you may overflow*
> *with hope by the power of the Holy Spirit."*
> *Romans 15:13 (NIV)*

Due to the heartbreaks in Bunni's life, she has compassion and empathy for hurting people. She knows what it feels like to suffer through heartbreaks, betrayals, and loss. She also understands the importance and value of friends. Bunni does her best to encourage, comfort, and love people whenever possible. Satan strived to break her spirit many times, but God used her heartbreaks to touch many lives.

> *"You intended to harm me, but God intended it*
> *for good to accomplish what is now being done,*
> *the saving of many lives." Genesis 50:20 (NIV)*

One friend shared, "No matter what Bunni is doing, she will stop to pray with you, help you, or give you a big hug. Bunni is a true friend." One of her adopted nephews said, "I love my Aunt Bunni. She encourages me, gives me hugs, and loves me unconditionally. I'm blessed to have her in my life." And another friend shared, "When Bunni arrives, she lights up the room. You can see God's love shining through her smile and actions. Her energy is infectious! I'm grateful she is my friend."

In closing, we will have "ups and downs" during our lifetime — but if you embrace God's promises and love others, your life can be filled with joy and happiness. Bunni chose to hold on to God's promises, unconditionally love others, and not allow heartbreaks to define her life. She shared, "Life may give you lemons, but through God's love and peace, you can make lemonade!"

Bunni

REFLECTION

As we saw in Bunni's story, life turned out much different than she hoped or imagined. Thankfully, throughout her journey, God placed "the right people" in her life just when she needed them. Friends and family carried her through many tough times and rejoiced with her during the good times.

Pause and Reflect.

1. Has God placed people in your life at just the right time? What happened?

_____

_____

_____

_____

_____

_____

_____

2. Are you embracing the positive things in your life, or are you stuck in the heartbreaks from your past?

_____

_____

_____

_____

_____

_____

_____

3. With God's love, direction, and peace, Bunni turned life's lemons into lemonade. Take a moment and list the "lemons" in your life (e.g., heartbreaks, challenges, fears, failures, etc.). Do you want to surrender your "lemons" to God, so He can help you make "lemonade" and move forward with your life?

    _____

    _____

    _____

    _____

    _____

    _____

    _____

NEXT STEPS

Friends are a gift from God. Take a moment and reflect on the friendships in your life.

1. List seven attributes of a good friend:

    *   _____

    *   _____

    *   _____

    *   _____

    *   _____

    *   _____

    *   _____

2. Based on the attributes you listed above, are you a good friend?

_____

_____

_____

_____

3. What three things can you do to be a better friend?

- _____

- _____

- _____

CLOSING PRAYER

Dear Heavenly Father,

Please help me to be a good friend who shares the "Fruit of the Spirit" with others.

> *"But the fruit of the Spirit is love, joy, peace,*
> *patience, kindness, goodness, faithfulness,*
> *gentleness, and self-control." Galatians 5:22-24 (NIV)*

Thank you for the gift of friendship. I love you. Amen!

My Child is a Drug Addict

Immediately the boy's father exclaimed,
"I do believe; help me overcome my unbelief!"
Mark 9:24 (NIV)

It was the middle of the night. Stella was alone in a hotel room when her cell phone unexpectedly rang. As she picked up the phone, her son's friend frantically blurted out, "Alex overdosed. He was purple and not breathing. He's been rushed to the hospital." Stella panicked. Her son was only twenty years old and 1500 miles away. What was she going to do?

Stella was born into an affluent, atheist family. Her mother was a successful writer for the Federal Government, and her father enjoyed a gratifying career in the military. Unfortunately, their polished outward appearances masked a dysfunctional home life, fraught with secrets and facades. Her parents were closet alcoholics.

Stella's earliest memories of her family surround alcohol and pills. As she describes it, "My mother was an alcoholic who functioned during the day, and binge drank at night. Mom would buy a bottle of booze from the local liquor store on her way home, and we would find the empty bottle at the bottom of her bed the next morning." Stella portrays her father as a "hardcore drunk." Life was not easy. At age four, her parents divorced. She continued living with her mother and rarely saw her father since he deployed overseas.

While growing up, her mother spoke openly about her disbelief in God and poked fun at people with faith. Stella frequently heard that faith was stupid. Her mother would boldly state, "You need to be strong! Religion is for weak and sick people." Despite her mother's outspoken comments, Stella silently desired to go to church and occasionally attended with friends. Sometimes her mother would use the church as a convenience since she was a single mom. She would drop Stella off at the church on a Sunday morning, then go to the store or take care of errands.

As the years went by, her mom married and divorced again. As her mother's drinking continued, Stella became angry. "I was ashamed of my Mom — her drinking embarrassed me." However, she lived in a culture of appearances, so Stella learned to hide her feelings and problems, a pattern that would haunt her as an adult. She remembers thinking, "Money cannot buy happiness — there are a lot of miserable rich people. There must be more to life."

"For where your treasure is, there your heart will be also."
Matthew 6:21 (NIV)

Stella attended an elite high school, where many kids drove expensive cars, and there was a high rate of drug use. During high school and continuing through college, Stella partied with her friends, which included drinking alcohol and smoking pot. Simply stated, she was a party girl following in her mother's footsteps. Despite her active social life, she was able to function and make good grades. While in high school, Stella met a young man from an elite and wealthy family. Ryan was extremely popular, but he had a secret — he was a functioning alcoholic. They soon became high school sweethearts and continued to date once they went to college.

While attending college, Stella found herself yearning for something bigger than herself. She pursued a minor in religion, as she searched to understand life. After graduation, Stella accepted Ryan's marriage proposal, fully aware that he had a significant drinking problem. She hoped once they were married and had children, his drinking would settle down, and they could enjoy a "normal life." She had seen firsthand the damage alcohol could bring to a family, but buried her fears and moved forward.

Two years after they were married, they welcomed a beautiful son into their lives named Alex, followed by the birth of a daughter a few years later. Stella was building a successful career while her husband continued to drink. He drank from the moment he woke up until he passed out or went to bed. Since she learned to bury issues and maintain a public façade, Stella pressed forward, working full time while trying to hold her family together. As time passed, they welcomed another daughter into their family.

By this time, Stella was overwhelmed. She had no help or support. Ryan would drink between 24-40 beers a day and received multiple DUIs. Her mother and his family provided no encouragement or relief. Life was horrible, and she was exhausted. Finally, after twelve years of marriage, Stella gave Ryan an ultimatum. "You have three months to stop drinking, or I'm leaving with the children." After ninety days passed, his decision was clear, "He chose a bottle of booze over the kids and me." She thought alcoholism was a choice and did not view it as a disease.

All alone, Stella packed up the kids, found a townhouse about forty-five minutes away, and attempted to create a healthy home environment for her children. She enrolled the kids in new schools and a variety of afterschool activities, sought family counseling, and filed for divorce. For the next two years, they survived on her salary with no child support.

> "...and call on me in the day of trouble;
> I will deliver you, and you will honor me."
> Psalm 50:15 (NIV)

Stella was overwhelmed as she desperately tried to keep her head above water. She was a single Mom trying to care for her children while "holding on" to a demanding job. There was no family to reach out to for support, and her friends from the old neighborhood lived too far away to help with day-to-day challenges. She was exhausted. Her estranged husband provided no assistance, and she was nervous to engage him due to his continued drinking. Stella felt isolated, unworthy, and alone. She did her best to press forward, believing there was nowhere to turn for assistance.

> "Come to me, all you who are weary and burdened,
> and I will give you rest." Matthew 11:28 (NIV)

As time passed, Stella started to experience challenges with her son Alex. He was diagnosed with Tourette's Syndrome and was embarrassed by the resulting "tics" in his face. The involuntary twitches caused him to "squish-up" his face and make odd facial expressions. Despite his challenges and the social pressures associated with it, Alex was making good grades. He was artistic, smart, and involved with sports. Stella had big dreams for his future.

Unfortunately, as Alex grew older, he felt increasingly awkward. He struggled to deal with his emotions and to "fit in." He had outbursts and "threw fits" as a way to express himself. Stella loved her son, and her heart broke for him. She did her best to help him adjust to peer pressures while supporting her two daughters and working full time to pay the bills.

"Cast your cares on the Lord
and he will sustain you..." Psalm 55:22 (NIV)

By age twelve, Alex's anger grew, and his outbursts became more violent. Stella believed he was disobedient, so she sought the help of a psychologist. Regrettably, she soon discovered Alex was secretly drinking and abusing cough syrup and other types of over-the-counter medication. She was shocked, devastated, and felt like a failure. Stella was drowning in guilt and demoralized by the situation. She blamed herself, felt unworthy, and routinely "beat herself up," thinking, "I'm a terrible Mom. Perhaps I should have stayed with the kid's Dad. What have I done?"

"We are hard-pressed on every side, but not crushed;
perplexed, but not in despair; persecuted, but not abandoned;
struck down, but not destroyed." 2 Corinthians 4:8-9 (NIV)

When Alex turned thirteen, he began to experience routine run-ins with the police. His drinking intensified, and he regularly used marijuana. Before long, Alex started to run away from home and ditch school. To make matters worse, he was failing his Freshmen classes. Stella feared he would never graduate from high school, but she soon learned this was the least of her problems.

Within a short time, Stella's father passed away, followed by the death of her mother. Desperate for some balance in their lives, Stella reluctantly asked her ex-husband if Alex could move in with him. Unfortunately, this complicated the situation and escalated Alex's drug use. She later learned her "ex" allowed Alex to smoke and drink alcohol in his home, which intensified the problem. She had no choice but to move Alex back home.

By age fourteen, Alex was in a death spiral. To support his drug habit, he started to shoplift and steal money, tools, jewelry, and electronics from their home. His violent outbursts became a regular occurrence. Stella was afraid of her son and feared for the safety of her daughters. For the girls' protection, she developed the code word "birdcage," which meant they should immediately leave the house and go to a neighbor's home if she felt they were in danger.

"The Lord is a refuge for the oppressed,
a stronghold in times of trouble." Psalm 9:9 (NIV)

Due to numerous issues, the courts sent Alex to the County Juvenile Detention Center. Fearing for her son's future, Stella dipped into her retirement savings to seek professional legal assistance. Her goal was to move him to another location versus being locked up in the detention center. Soon, via court order, Alex was released to a private boarding school for at-risk teenagers about 500 miles away. Despite being financially strapped, Stella paid for the expensive school. To her dismay, she received a call within the first week, stating he ran away. The school classified Alex as an "extreme at-risk kid."

"Do not let your hearts be troubled.
You believe in God; believe also in me." John 14:1 (NIV)

The boarding school recommended that Stella immediately place Alex into a structured wilderness program for troubled teens. She paid an additional $35,000 to enroll him in the program, then hoped for the best. Alex celebrated his fifteenth birthday in the wilderness, away from his family and friends. Fortunately, through the program, he began to rebuild his self-esteem, develop new skills, and gain a fresh perspective about his life. After several months, he was able to return to the boarding school. There was hope.

For the next ten months, Alex made progress. He caught up on the classes he failed the prior school year and participated in counseling. He was diagnosed with a bipolar disorder and placed on several medications, which seemed to make a difference. It was during this time, the school informed Stella that her son was an addict, but she was in denial and thought, "Alex has used drugs, but he isn't an addict – addicts are hopeless, they live on the streets, they aren't loved." She was blind to reality, as she frantically tried to hold her family together and get her son through high school.

Then one night, Alex broke a school window and ran away again. Stella feared her son might die as he roamed the streets alone, at the age of sixteen. To complicate the situation, the boarding school permanently kicked Alex out of their program. Despite the gravity of the situation, Stella still did not fully grasp his drug problem.

Authorities finally located Alex the following day, so Stella made the 500-mile drive to pick him up and bring him home. Within months, Alex was arrested once again and placed on probation. Stella frantically worked with the police, county, local school, and family counselor to stabilize his latest crisis, but the situation was overwhelming.

> *"Peace I leave with you; my peace I give you.*
> *I do not give to you as the world gives.*
> *Do not let your hearts be troubled*
> *and do not be afraid." John 14:27 (NIV)*

Then, there was a glimmer of hope, just before his senior year. Alex began to make new friends and claimed he was attending 12-step meetings for recovering addicts. Stella thought they finally turned a major corner, but within a few months, everything came crashing down once again.

She discovered her son was shooting heroin. When she thought Alex was attending 12-step meetings, he was buying drugs with his friends in another town. He was a heroin addict but would also use any drugs he could get his hands on, including crack cocaine, methamphetamines, and ecstasy. Stella quickly abandoned her dream of his high school graduation as she focused on saving her son from an overdose.

She soon learned Alex was stealing checks out of the middle of her checkbook to obtain cash for drugs. He also pawned her jewelry, including sentimental pieces from her deceased mother and grandmother, and other items belonging to the family. He sold anything of value for drugs. Blinded by her drive to save her son, Stella dipped into her retirement funds once again and placed Alex into one rehab facility and then another, but nothing worked.

Stella was falling apart and feared Alex would die. She panicked every time the phone rang. When there was a siren in the distance, she would cover her ears with her hands and close her eyes, trying to make the sound go away. Her daughters were angry and concerned by the constant turmoil surrounding their mother and brother. Peace and calm eluded her entire family, which was now surrounded by continuous stress and turbulence. Stella finally opened up, and confidentially shared Alex's situation with her boss. She could no longer carry this secret by herself. He empathetically embraced and supported her, granting her time off during the day with the ability to sometimes work from home. She was grateful.

"Carry each other's burdens, and in this way
you will fulfill the law of Christ." Galatians 6:2 (NIV)

Then, one October night, at the age of eighteen, Alex overdosed while staying with his father. When the ambulance arrived, the emergency technicians worked hard to revive him, then rushed him to the hospital. Stella panicked when she received the call and raced to be by his side, hoping for the best but fearing the worst.

Upon arriving at the hospital, Stella was relieved and grateful to learn Alex survived and would be okay. Then, the doctor said, "Unfortunately, your son does not want to see you." Confused and heartbroken, Stella was overpowered with emotions and fell apart. Despite her fragile and exhausted state, she pulled herself together with the help of her daughters. She had to remain strong to save her son and strive to be the best mother possible for her daughters.

The next months were chaotic. The police arrested Alex for probation violations and felony possession of drugs. The court sentenced him to seven months in jail, followed by rehab once again. The following year, he faced additional probation violations but fled more than 1500 miles to avoid jail. Alex claimed he had a job and was living with a friend.

During this time, Stella decided the girls needed a fresh start, so she transitioned her job to another state. To her surprise, she soon met a remarkable man, and they were married. This unexpected marriage brought stability and calmness to their lives. Her husband understood the pain, suffering, and disappointments they had lived through because he was a recovering addict. He surrounded Stella and the girls with compassion, empathy, and understanding regarding Alex and their experiences with his addiction. They were thankful.

Stella continued to work full time. Due to her high-profile work projects, she periodically traveled to brief the Sector President and his staff. One day in June, she flew to the corporate office, checked into a hotel, finished preparations for her morning briefing, and went to bed. Suddenly at 4:00 AM ET, her cell phone rang. It was Alex's roommate. As Stella pulled the phone to her ear, she heard, "Alex overdosed. He was purple and not breathing. He's been rushed to the hospital." He had no further information.

Stunned and panicked, Stella went into research mode, trying to get information about Alex. When she called the local hospital, they refused to release any information. She begged, "Can you please, at least tell me if my son is alive or dead?" The hospital stated they were unable to share information and suggested she call the local coroner.

Terrified, Stella called the police department. The information officer stated, "Someone fitting your son's description has been arrested. You can check the morning booking report to find out if it was your son, it is published at 6:00 AM MT." The next hours were painful and agonizing as she feared the worst. Somehow she pulled herself together, showered, and dressed to prepare for her morning briefing. Then an odd thing occurred. As the clock ticked closer to 8:00 AM (6:00 AM MT), she sensed things would be okay. When the police booking report was finally available, she learned Alex was alive and under arrest for drug possession.

Grateful that Alex was alive, Stella drove to the morning meeting, delivered her presentation, and handled questions — never divulging her horrific night or the fears she was facing. After a long day, she returned to the solitude of her hotel room. That night, Stella, who was raised in an atheist home, got down on her hands and knees, then started to pray to God. Sobbing, she said, "God, I don't know who you are. I don't even know if you are real, but I need you to save my son."

"Hear my prayer, Lord, listen to my cry for help;
do not be deaf to my weeping..." Psalm 39:12 (NIV)

Stella bailed her son out of jail once again, but he was soon arrested for a robbery associated with a "bad drug deal." This time, the court sentenced him to eighteen months in the county jail. Stella realized her hands were tied. She knew he was safe in jail, so she decided to embrace this time to heal and began attending Al-Anon meetings at a nearby church. Before long, she was going to church every Sunday with her family.

Then, one Sunday morning, the pastor spoke on "The Blessings of Rain." He shared, "Sometimes life has one storm after another, but during our storms, we need to have faith in God. He will carry us through our tough times if we keep trusting Him. Be patient! Eventually, flowers will grow, and sometimes there might even be a rainbow."

That evening, Stella stepped outside. To the right, she saw storm clouds with pouring rain. In front of her, the sun was starting to set, but on the left, she saw a vibrant, beautiful rainbow. Stella shared, "This was a powerful, life-changing moment for me. I made a personal connection with God and knew everything would be okay. Since this time, I have accepted that I am powerless and choose to place my trust in a power much bigger than me — God."

"So do not fear, for I am with you; do not be dismayed,
for I am your God. I will strengthen you and help you;
I will uphold you with my righteous right hand."
Isaiah 41:10 (NIV)

But Stella's story does not stop here. God has been working in the lives of her entire family. Her husband is very active in his 12-step recovery program, which includes taking 12-step meetings into jails, rehab centers, and homeless shelters. After some turbulent times, her oldest daughter found the love of Jesus and is now a missionary. She has traveled to several countries to help people overcome addictions and escape human trafficking. Her youngest daughter is attending a Christian school and loves the Lord.

> *"Finally, be strong in the Lord and in his mighty power."*
> *Ephesians 6:10 (NIV)*

For many months Alex lived in a homeless shelter just five miles from their home. During his ten plus years of addiction, he has overdosed over twenty times, but Stella believes as long as Alex is breathing, there is hope. She has learned to accept his addiction, and love him the best she can, without enabling his addiction.

Alex finally checked into a homeless treatment center and stayed until he graduated from their 30-day recovery program. After graduation, he transitioned to a faith-based recovery home, where he attends church and bible-study regularly and is active in 12-step recovery. While Stella realizes a relapse is possible, especially in early recovery, she takes comfort in knowing God's will is at work, and there is no greater love. Stella sees Alex regularly, prays for him to continue on his current path, and thanks God for every day that he remains clean and sober. Alex recently told her, "God has a plan for me — He wants me here."

Stella quit her demanding job and now consults for various businesses. Her primary focus is to help families of addicts. She supports a weekly radio show focused on raising awareness of addiction and opportunities for recovery. Stella is also active in Nar-Anon (a 12-step program for the loved ones of addicts) and supports Christian Sober Homes by volunteering, advocating, and securing donations. She shared, "Many people are struggling with addictions — men, women, young, old, rich, and poor. We need to love people and not judge them. Addiction is a disease and not a moral failing. Don't be ashamed to talk about it."

In closing, Stella is now at peace and no longer living a dual life. She shared, "I decided to remove my mask and live a transparent life. Through our storms, I met my husband, and I met God, who taught me lessons in love, tolerance, and compassion. Before God, I was judgemental. I now have the grace to love, even the most broken people in this world. I will forever be grateful." She recently had a tattoo placed on her arm, which says, "Let Go, Let God!"

Never stop believing in the power and love of God. He is with us and for us! Amen.

> *"But those who hope in the Lord will renew their strength.*
> *They will soar on wings like eagles;*
> *they will run and not grow weary;*
> *they will walk and not be faint." Isaiah 40:31 (NIV)*

Author's Note:

At the beginning of Alex's challenges, Stella began to notice the time 9:24 on her clock several times a week. She shared, "At first, I thought it was neat because 9:24 is my mother's birthday." However, as she continued to see 9:24 month after month, she began to think it was rather odd. 9:24 soon became a topic of conversation between her co-workers and daughters; they would text or call Stella when they saw it. This unexplained pattern continued for ten years.

Then, a few years ago, she was emailing a gratitude list, when she noticed one friend had "9:24 — I believe, help my unbelief" under her name. Stella immediately took a picture of her computer screen and asked her friend, "What is this?". She was blown away by the answer, "Oh, that is from the powerful Bible verse Mark 9:24. When Stella looked up the Bible verse, she was astounded and filled with love for our Heavenly Father. The Bible verse states:

> *"Immediately the boy's father exclaimed,*
> *I do believe; help me overcome my unbelief!"*
> *Mark 9:24 (NIV)*

This verse "summed up" Stella's journey, and she claims Mark 9:24 as "My God Wink" and life verse. She now fully grasps that God was with her the entire time — she just needed to recognize Him, embrace Him, and believe.

REFLECTION

As we saw in Stella's story, addictions negatively impact entire families. If your family is affected by alcoholism or drug abuse, do not be embarrassed to ask for help, whether it be for yourself or a loved one. Be transparent as you shine light into the darkness. God will be with you.

1. Pause and Reflect. Do you worry about a friend or family member who is drinking too much? Are you drinking too much? Are you pretending a drug addiction does not exist? Do you feel compelled to lie for someone or "cover-up" an addiction issue?

   If you answered "Yes" to any of these questions, there is good news. You can reach out for help right now by following the "Next Steps."

   _____

   _____

   _____

   _____

   _____

2. Are you carrying scars from living with an addict now or in the past? If you answered, "Yes," embrace one of the "Next Steps."

   _____

   _____

   _____

   _____

   _____

   _____

NEXT STEPS

There are a variety of resources and support groups to help addicts and the families of addicts. If you want or need to seek professional help for yourself or a loved one, below are some contacts and resources. Remember, you are not alone!

- SAMHSA National Helpline for Substance Abuse and Treatment 24/7 1-800-662-HELP (4357)
- Celebrate Recovery https://www.celebraterecovery.com
- Narcotics Anonymous https://www.na.org/
- Nar-Anon for Families and Friends of Addicts https://www.nar-anon.org/
- Alcoholics Anonymous® http://www.aa.org
- Al-Anon® for Families and Friends of Alcoholics https://al-anon.org
- Alateen® https://al-anon.org/for-members/group-resources/alateen/
- NOPE (Narcotics Overdose Prevention & Education) http://www.nopetaskforce.org/
- Local Women Centers
- Homeless Shelters
- Employee Assistance Programs through your employer
- Your Pastor, Minister, or Priest
- Your doctor, local hospital, or community church can provide you with a list of counselors if you want or need help.
- Family Members or Friends

CLOSING PRAYER

Dear Heavenly Father,

Thank you for your love, grace, and compassion! Please help _____ to recognize, seek help, and overcome my/his/her addiction. I know this will be a long journey, but with you, all things are possible. Please provide me with the strength and guidance I need to persevere through this journey. To God, be the glory! Amen

Healed Through the Grace of God

"But when you ask, you must believe and not doubt,
because the one who doubts is like a wave of the sea,
blown and tossed by the wind." James 1:6 (NIV)

The doctors and nurses frantically ran beside Heather's gurney; time was working against them. Suddenly, there was a loud bang as they pushed her gurney through the double doors, on the way to the operating room. Then, without warning, a nurse thrust Heather's tennis shoes, jewelry, and a piece of clothing into her mother's arms and said, "Here — These are hers. Hurry — tell her goodbye." The doctors paused for a brief moment so her parents could say their goodbyes, then rushed Heather into surgery.

Heather grew up in a small town in Louisiana and was the only child of Darrell and Jenny Gilbert. She was a remarkable daughter and enjoyed a great relationship with her parents and grandparents. The family's faith in God sustained them through the ups and downs in life, but they had no idea what a critical role their faith would play in Heather's future.

From an early age, it was quite clear that Heather was destined for great things. She was a beautiful girl, both inside and out, and God blessed her with an amazing singing voice. By the age of ten, she was comfortable with public appearances and performances ranging from singing engagements to stage productions and pageants.

By the time Heather became a teenager, she had over one-hundred pageant titles, released her first country album, and was the talent winner for the National "Little Miss America" pageant. She was a very busy young lady. As she began to focus on high school, Heather made a conscious decision to reduce her professional appearances so she could enjoy school activities and her friends.

Heather was popular in high school and was excited to be part of the cheerleading squad. Life was great, and her future was promising. As she strived for more independence, her parents gave her a car during her junior year in high school, but the car came with a clear stipulation. Since she was a relatively new driver, she could not drive to school until after spring break. Heather was excited about her car, but carefully adhered to her parent's rules.

Then one beautiful April morning, just before spring break, Heather finished getting ready for school. She made sure her blonde hair was just right and gave her vibrant blue eyes one more sweep of mascara. It was a particularly exciting morning, as her mother was busy packing and preparing for their upcoming family vacation to the Cayman Islands.

Heather wanted to take her car to school that day, so she begged her Mom to bend their rules. "Mom, you have so much to do to get ready for our trip, can I please, please drive my car to school? After all, it's just a straight shot to the high school, and I will be fine." Initially, her mother said, "no." But after some back and forth conversations, her parents gave in and allowed their daughter to drive the car.

Heather's father, Darrell, was working at the local gas refinery that morning when he heard a loud crash in the distance. As his heart pounded, he jumped in his car and drove less than a mile, until he came upon a horrific accident on the two-lane road close to their home — a head-on collision between an eighteen-wheeler truck and a white car. He immediately realized the crushed and mangled car belonged to Heather.

Darrell was the first person to arrive at the scene of the accident. Panicked, he rushed out of his car to help his daughter. Heather was wedged in the car — her eyes were open, but she did not respond to his voice. Within a few minutes, the fire department arrived and pulled Darrell away from the wreckage so they could attempt to save his daughter.

The firemen carefully used the "jaws of life" to remove her from the car, realizing time was of the essence. Heather was in critical condition as the paramedics frantically tried to stabilize her. She was non-responsive when they loaded her into the ambulance and rushed her to the local hospital, about ten minutes away. The truck driver was not injured.

The news about the accident quickly spread throughout the small town, and people began to gather at the site of the crash. As Darrell rushed to the hospital, his best friend went to pick up Heather's mother, Jenny. When his friend arrived at their home, he calmly said, "Darrell sent me to get you. Get your purse, and we need to go."

Jenny immediately knew something was terribly wrong as she grabbed her purse. Her body felt as if it was shutting down and going into a "protective mode." Perhaps it was the shock of the odd situation or God's way of protecting her from the events that would soon unfold. She remembers bracing herself, thinking something happened to her husband Darrell while he was working at the local gas plant. Jenny began to pray quietly.

As they drove toward the hospital, they passed the site of the accident, and Jenny saw Heather's car. The car was crushed, and the car door was off. She suddenly thought, "Oh, God! This is not about Darrell — this is about my child." Jenny then prayed, "Father, please let her be okay."

> *"Then you will call on me and come and pray to me,*
> *and I will listen to you." Jeremiah 29:12 (NIV)*

When they arrived at the small hospital, the waiting room was chaotic. Neighbors, school friends, and Darrell's co-workers gathered together while the doctors desperately tried to stabilize Heather, but the hospital was not equipped to handle her significant injuries. As the doctors anxiously waited for a medivac helicopter to arrive, they allowed Darrell and Jenny to spend a few moments with their daughter.

Jenny tried to keep herself together as they walked into the emergency room. Heather slipped in and out of consciousness but realized her parents were there. "I can't see. I can't see. Everything is black." As they lovingly held their daughter's hands to comfort her, Darrell silently prayed over his daughter. Then Heather whispered, "Pray for me. Sing to me." Jenny immediately leaned down so her daughter could hear her voice as she prayed.

> *"I call on you, my God, for you will answer me;*
> *turn your ear to me and hear my prayer."*
> *Psalm 17:6 (NIV)*

Heather had a broken nose, there was a large gash on her forehead, and her hair was full of broken glass, but they did not fully grasp the extent of their daughter's injuries. Heather was in excruciating pain, and her blood pressure was dropping. As they did their best to console their daughter, one of her doctors anxiously waited for the helicopter and kept saying, "What is taking so long? What is taking so long?"

When they finally heard the helicopter land, Darrell and Jenny told Heather they loved her, then left the room as the doctors made final preparations for her flight to the critical care center about sixty miles away. As the helicopter flew off, Darrell's brother Bobby and his wife Carol quickly drove Heather's parents to the Shreveport Christus Catholic Hospital.

As her parents ran into the emergency center, a team of doctors and nurses were already desperately working on Heather. Darrell and Jenny were overwhelmed as hospital officials began thrusting papers and legal documents in front of them to sign. Then one office manager compassionately said, "Hurry, you need to hurry. Just sign here."

Suddenly, there was a loud bang as a team of doctors and nurses pushed Heather's gurney through the double doors, on the way to the operating room. Then, without warning, a nurse thrust

Heather's tennis shoes, jewelry, and a piece of clothing into her mother's arms and said, "Here — These are hers. Hurry — tell her goodbye." The doctors paused for a brief moment so her parents could kiss her hands and say, "We love you. You will be okay. We will be here waiting for you." Then a doctor said, "We have got to go."

"And now these three remain: faith, hope, and love.
But the greatest of these is love." 1 Corinthians 13:13 (NIV)

As they quickly rolled Heather into surgery, Darrell and Jenny realized this could be it, and they both started to cry. Thankfully, a priest and a nun saw what was transpiring and suggested they go into the chapel to pray. Bobby and Carol joined them. As they knelt, they started to sob as the priest prayed, and the nun consoled them.

"For where two or three gather in my name,
there am I with them." Matthew 18:20 (NIV)

Then, the first of a series of miracles occurred. Right in the middle of praying and crying, Bobby, a man of few words, suddenly spoke out, and said with his deep voice, "Listen, did you hear that voice? You guys, listen. The voice, the voice spoke – it's in my ears. I think it's God. I'm amazed you didn't hear it." Carol immediately tried to console her husband and said, "Honey, you are just in shock."

But Bobby knew what he heard and became adamant. Then God whispered to him once again, "They cannot hear me. Tell them. She will survive. She will be alright." As Bobby loudly proclaimed the words that God gave him, the priest stopped praying, then said, "Praise God." At that moment, both Jenny and Darrell stopped crying, got off their knees, and sat on the pew. They felt God's indescribable peace and love surrounding them and immediately knew Heather would be okay.

"And the peace of God, which transcends all understanding,
will guard your hearts and your minds in Christ Jesus."
Philippians 4:7 (NIV)

After a few long hours, two doctors emerged from the operating room and shared that Heather survived the first of many surgeries. Their primary focus at this point was to stabilize her condition. Then the lead doctors stated, "Heather suffered significant trauma. When she came in, there was a low probability she would survive. We thought her liver burst due to the impact of the accident. But there is some good news, Heather's spleen burst, not her liver. The remarkable thing is that we have a first. Heather has an extra spleen so it can keep doing its job. People don't usually have spare parts."

*Jesus replied, "What is impossible with man
is possible with God." Luke 18:27 (NIV)*

The younger doctor appeared restless during the conversation, then said, "Shall we discuss what happened during her surgery? At that point, the older doctor shared, "Heather had quite a religious experience in the operating room, and we did too. I believe when something spiritual happens, it is a good practice to let the individual keep that between themselves and God." No other details were shared. There was a pause in the conversation, then Jenny said, "We just had our own experience in the chapel."

*"Peace I leave with you; my peace I give you.
I do not give to you as the world gives.
Do not let your hearts be troubled
and do not be afraid." John 14:27 (NIV)*

Due to her significant injuries and pain, Heather was placed in a drug-induced coma so her body could heal. Jenny stayed with her daughter, both night and day, as the family continued to pray for her complete recovery. It was during this critical time that a special nun began to visit Heather's room very early each morning. Jenny said, "This nun was beautiful and had vibrant blue eyes. She dressed in a white vintage habit. She would quietly walk into Heather's room, hold her hand, then recite the Lord's Prayer, before silently leaving. No other words were ever shared."

Within a few days, the doctors began to wake Heather up to prepare her for the next set of surgeries. Gratefully, when she opened her eyes, her sight returned, and she recognized her family. As Heather started to talk in small increments, she would recite the Lord's Prayer with the nun early each morning. This angelic nun provided incredible comfort, and she was a blessing from God.

The Lord's Prayer
Matthew 6:9-13

Our Father who art in heaven, Hallowed be thy name.
Thy kingdom come,
Thy will be done on earth, as it is in heaven.
Give us this day our daily bread.
And forgive us our trespasses,
as we forgive those who trespass against us.
And lead us not into temptation, but deliver us from evil.
For thine is the kingdom, and the power,
and the glory, for ever and ever. Amen.

Over the next week, Heather endured two painful surgeries to fix her broken hip and crushed ankle. Unfortunately, as the days progressed, she developed a fever. Despite bombarding her body with antibiotics, the doctors were unable to locate the source of her infection. Heather deteriorated quickly despite their efforts to change her medications.

Then one night, when Heather was extremely ill, she said, "Mother, I want you to go get the nun in white. I want her to pray for my infection." Heather was persistent, so Jenny walked out to the nurse's station and asked, "Can we please have the nun in white, who comes in early in the morning, come pray with my daughter?" Jenny was shocked when the nurses replied, "We're sorry, but we are confused. We do not have a nun who wears white or comes in early in the morning."

With that shocking revelation, Jenny went to the chapel to pray. Then, a remarkable thing happened. The nun dressed in white reappeared. She quietly walked into Heather's room, held her hand, and once again recited the Lord's Prayer. But this time, before she left, she carefully touched Heather's hip, then quietly left the room.

Heather smiled, then said to her Mom, "Good. I'm glad she came in." Jenny and Heather cannot explain what happened, but they both know God was in control.

"Praise be to the God and Father of our Lord Jesus Christ,
the Father of compassion and the God of all comfort."
2 Corinthians 1:3 (NIV)

When the doctor examined Heather the next morning, there was a large blister where the nun had gently laid her hand the night before. When the doctor touched the blister, it opened, and a foul-smelling infection began to drain out of Heather's body. Heather's fever soon disappeared, and the infection was gone. They never saw the nun again.

Heather remained in the hospital for two long, painful months. During this time, she lost thirty pounds and was confined to her bed and a wheelchair. At age seventeen, she endured excruciating pain as they hoisted her out of bed each morning for physical therapy. Despite the grueling treatments, Heather and her family continued to focus on God's promises. They knew God had a plan for Heather's life. After all, it was a miracle she was even alive.

"For I know the plans I have for you," declares the Lord,
"plans to prosper you and not to harm you,
plans to give you hope and a future." Jeremiah 29:11 (NIV)

Unfortunately, as the days passed, her doctor shared some disheartening news. In addition to Heather's internal injuries, hip fracture, and crushed ankle, her other foot suffered significant nerve damage and was considered a "dead foot." Her primary doctor told Heather she would probably never walk again or have children. Heather was afraid, but Jenny and Darrell refused to accept the latest news and kept trusting God.

That night, Darrell, Jenny, and Heather's nurse gathered around her bed. They were committed to remain positive and keep trusting God. Holding hands, they prayed over Heather's "dead foot" and asked God to restore Heather's foot so she could walk again.

The next morning Heather's doctor came in and said, "I could not sleep last night. I kept thinking about your foot. There is one more thing that might be causing your "dead foot." Because you have so much faith, I am going to take you back into surgery to determine if there is a bone fragment placing pressure on the nerves."

> *"Now, faith is confidence in what we hope for*
> *and assurance about what we do not see."*
> *Hebrews 11:1 (NIV)*

The next day, Heather was wheeled into surgery once again. When the surgical procedure was over, the doctor walked out of the operating room with a big smile on his face and said, "We got it. There was a little bone fragment "cutting-off" the feeling in her foot. Her foot should make a full recovery." Heather and her parents lifted-up prayers of thanksgiving and kept looking forward.

Heather was now a skeleton of her former self. Her lack of strength and endurance was an ongoing challenge. Despite her physical condition, she was unwilling to "give up." Finally, after weeks of agonizing physical therapy, she was able to bear some weight on her legs. Although it was painful, her family, doctors, and nurses rejoiced when she had this breakthrough. Heather was committed and said, "I will walk and cheer again!"

> *"Have I not commanded you? Be strong and courageous.*
> *Do not be afraid; do not be discouraged, for the Lord*
> *your God will be with you wherever you go."*
> *Joshua 1:9 (NIV)*

When the doctors finally released Heather from the hospital, her parents built a wheelchair ramp at their home and brought in a hospital bed. Heather faithfully continued her extensive physical therapy program, committed to a full recovery. Over the summer, she slowly graduated from her wheelchair to a walker, and then a balance cane. Before long, Heather was walking without assistance.

When the fall semester arrived, Heather returned to school on a full-time basis. And then, an incredible thing happened. She rejoined the cheerleading team. Thanks to some simple cheer routines, Heather was able to work around her hip and ankle challenges. That spring, she graduated with the rest of her class and walked across the stage to accept her diploma. God continued to bless and protect her over the following years, and she was grateful. Heather eventually married, and God blessed her with a beautiful baby girl.

Several years after the accident, Heather was at a different hospital to complete some paperwork for an upcoming procedure. A nurse kept watching her, so Heather decided to say hello. It was at that point, the nurse shared, "I recognize you. You're a miracle. I was working in the operating room the day you came in — you were one of my first cases. You were so young, and your chances were not good."

Romans 8:38-39 (NIV)

......Neither death nor life, neither angels nor demons,
neither the present nor the future, nor any powers,
neither height nor depth, nor anything else in all creation,
will be able to separate us from the
love of God that is in Christ Jesus our Lord.

Heather was curious, so she asked the nurse if she happened to remember what transpired in the operating room. The nurse shared, "Oh, yes. I will never forget. While you were under anesthesia, the doctors and nurses were frantically trying to save your life. Suddenly, you started to have a very vocal conversation with God. As the conversation continued, a cold breeze came through the room. The entire operating room was silent, and in awe of the religious experience we witnessed."

Isaiah 41:10 (NIV)

So do not fear, for I am with you;
do not be dismayed, for I am your God.
I will strengthen you and help you;
I will uphold you with my righteous right hand.

While reflecting on her life, Heather shared, "The accident and related events changed me forever. God literally showed me His power, compassion, and greatness. Through months of fear, pain, physical therapy, and uncertainty, God never left me."

"Throughout the different phases of my recovery, God allowed me to walk in many different shoes. He opened my eyes to the world around me. I now understand what it feels like to "face death head-on," and to hear the words — you may never walk again or have children. I experienced the helplessness of being bedridden, the frustrations of living in a wheelchair, and the heartbreak of being mocked by strangers as I struggled to accomplish the basic things in life. As a result of my experiences, God gave me the gift of empathy for others."

> *"Each of you should use whatever gift you have received to serve others, as faithful stewards of God's grace in its various forms." 1 Peter 4:10 (NIV)*

In closing, Heather shared, "I value the physical scars on my body as a daily reminder of God's miracles in my life. I no longer have a fear of death, for I know when my Heavenly Father is ready, He will call me home! In the meantime, I will do my best to fulfill His purpose for my life here on earth. I am grateful for each new day the Lord gives me."

Heather

REFLECTION

We live in a fallen world. Subsequently, unforeseen events can drastically alter our paths and plans. But — there is good news. No matter what challenges, adversities, or issues we face, God promises to be with us.

1. Have you dealt with challenges, adversities, or issue in your life? If yes, what happened? During your "tough times," did you ask God for strength and guidance?

_____

_____

_____

_____

_____

_____

2. No one can explain the appearance and disappearance of the nun in Heather's story. However, one thing we can be assured of, God comforts and cares for us in numerous ways. How has God comforted you?

_____

_____

_____

_____

_____

_____

NEXT STEPS

As we saw in Heather's story, prayer is powerful. The Bible reminds us:

> *"Do not be anxious about anything, but in every situation,*
> *by prayer and petition, with thanksgiving,*
> *present your requests to God." Philippians 4:6 (NIV)*

1. Sometimes, people think they need "special and fancy" words to talk with God, but that is not true. Prayer is simple. Just close your eyes and have a conversation with God. He is waiting to listen to you right now. What do you want Him to know?

   _____

   _____

   _____

   _____

   _____

2. What are some ways you can make prayer a centralized part of your life?

   _____

   _____

   _____

   _____

   _____

CLOSING PRAYER

Dear God,

Thank you for listening to me.
Thank you for helping me during my times of need.
Thank you for being a loving and compassionate Heavenly Father.
Thank you for _____. Amen.

Overcoming Bullying

*"Be joyful in hope, patient in affliction,
faithful in prayer." Romans 12:12 (NIV)*

Within a split second, Josie was on the floor in the school hallway. The verbal bullying finally escalated into a physical altercation. Stunned, embarrassed, and afraid, she picked herself up, brushed off her clothes, and headed to her next class. Josie tried to ignore the kids' comments and laughter as she walked away, but the words hurt and made her sad. She desperately wanted to "fit in" and have friends.

Josie was a bright, talkative little girl, full of curiosity and wonder. The world was like an empty slate, and she wanted to know all about it. Born in Brooklyn, New York, she was the oldest daughter of two loving parents who legally immigrated to America from the Caribbean. Her parents were grateful for the opportunities America offered, and they quickly rose to a "middle-class status" through hard work and sheer drive. They loved the Lord and raised their children in the Christian faith.

Josie was a thin, lanky child, and the youngest in her kindergarten class, but she always stood out due to her bright heritage clothing. She was fascinated with people and eager to know all about the kids in her class. Despite her outgoing personality, Josie had a hard time making friends in school, on the playground, and in her neighborhood — this confused her. At times, she felt sad playing by herself, but she learned to adapt.

> *"... 'Love your neighbor as yourself.'*
> *There is no commandment greater than these."*
> *Mark 12:31 (NIV)*

She attended a school in Brooklyn until the second grade when her family moved to the Long Island suburbs. The move was difficult on Josie as she tried to make friends and "fit in" to her new neighborhood and school. Since she was a curious child and fascinated with the other kids, she asked a lot of questions. Unfortunately, due to her inquisitive nature, the kids started to call her "Nosy Josie." The name hurt her feelings, and she began to think, "I wonder if it is wrong to ask questions and be curious. Maybe I need to change the way I act around people."

> *"Cast all your anxiety on Him*
> *because he cares for you."*
> *1 Peter 5:7 (NIV)*

Josie reflected, "As name calling and mean comments escalated throughout elementary school, I began to realize I might be different from the other kids based on my constant curiosity, how I dressed, the way I talked, and the color of my skin. I tried my best to "fit in" and be kind to all the kids, but I felt like an outsider. The kids excluded me. I felt lonely and isolated. I knew from the Bible that God loved all His children, and we were the same in His eyes, so why was this happening to me? Why was I being treated differently?"

> *"Do not be anxious about anything,*
> *but in every situation, by prayer and petition,*
> *with thanksgiving, present your requests to God."*
> *Philippians 4:6 (NIV)*

Josie continued, "On many occasions, I tried to tell my parents about the things going on at school and the way I felt. My parents were supportive, as they listened and loved me. But due to their upbringing, they lacked empathy and understanding regarding my perspective and thoughts."

Josie's parents were raised in a poverty-stricken country and extremely grateful for the opportunities America provided. They were thankful for the basics, such as employment, a roof over their heads, and food to eat. They knew first-hand what it felt like to endure extreme hardships and discrimination. They viewed Josie's concerns as minor issues when compared to the harsh environment they survived as children.

One time after Josie shared an issue that occurred at school, her mother said, "Why are you letting these people bother you?" When she heard these words come out of her mother's mouth, Josie immediately felt devalued and did not know how to respond. From that point forward, she began to internalize her feelings as she attempted to figure things out by herself.

> *"So do not fear, for I am with you;*
> *do not be dismayed, for I am your God.*
> *I will strengthen you and help you;*
> *I will uphold you with my righteous right hand."*
> *Isaiah 41:10 (NIV)*

Then one day, a teacher asked her, "Where are your parents from?" Little Josie quickly gave the teacher her home address. The teacher responded, "No, where are your parents from?" She then replied, "Oh, the Caribbean." The teacher then responded with a demeaning tone, "I could tell."

> *"...Believers in our glorious Lord Jesus Christ*
> *must not show favoritism."*
> *James 2:1 (NIV)*

Josie shared, "At that moment, my young mind was confused based on the teacher's response. I thought there was something wrong with me since my family came from a different country. I assumed this might be the reason I did not have friends. I believed I was 'not good enough,' and I was sad."

> *Then Peter began to speak: "I now realize how true it is that*
> *God does not show favoritism but accepts from every nation*

> *the one who fears him and does what is right."*
> *Acts 10:34-35 (NIV)*

Josie paused, took a breath, then said, "The comments from adults and children began to shape the way I viewed myself at age seven. I felt misunderstood and excluded. My feelings, emotional scars, and perceptions followed me into adulthood."

> *"Be strong and courageous. Do not be afraid or terrified*
> *because of them, for the Lord your God goes with you;*
> *he will never leave you nor forsake you."*
> *Deuteronomy 31:6 (NIV)*

In the third grade, Josie read *The Diary of Anne Frank*. The book was powerful and spoke to her heart. On some levels, she identified with Anne, as she longed to be like the other children. Anne Frank's Diary had a significant impact on her life.

As the months and years passed, Josie quietly endured bullying in a variety of forms, including threats, name-calling, cruel comments, and isolation. She believed in God and had a strong faith, but felt overwhelmed at times. Josie sought peace and safety in her mind, and discovered when she had a book to read — she always had a friend. Books provided a source of comfort and support, even though she was a slow reader.

> *"Even though I walk through the darkest valley,*
> *I will fear no evil, for you are with me;*
> *your rod and your staff, they comfort me."*
> *Psalm 23:4 (NIV)*

When Josie transitioned into junior high school, the devaluing comments, inconsiderate judgments, and name-calling escalated. The situation made her feel insecure while negatively impacting her self-esteem. She felt misunderstood, lacking positive feedback and validation from her peers, teachers, and parents. In an attempt to avoid the daily bullying, she did her best to stay out of everyone's way.

"Be kind and compassionate to one another..."
Ephesians 4:32 (NIV)

To make matters worse, Josie had eczema, and the kids made fun of her. Eczema is not contagious, but the students acted as if she had a disease so that she would be singled out and sent to the nurse's office. To get around the humiliation, Josie pretended to leave her gym clothes at home and skipped P.E. class, as often as possible. It was easier to be viewed as forgetful and dumb, versus mocked about her eczema.

As the bullying persisted, she began to struggle with math, in addition to her slow reading. Based on her academic and self-esteem challenges, Josie self-labeled herself as a poor student and an under-achiever. Due to her age and the situation, Josie did not fully grasp that she was special, God loved her, and He had a purpose for her life.

"For I know the plans I have for you," declares the Lord,
"plans to prosper you and not to harm you,
plans to give you hope and a future."
Jeremiah 29:11 (NIV)

As junior high school continued, there was a girl who relentlessly bullied Josie. After several weeks of verbal abuse, this girl began kicking her chair in class, pushing her in the hallways, and threatening to "beat her up." Afraid and intimidated, Josie believed she had nowhere to turn and desperately tried to figure a way out of her predicament, all by herself. At age twelve, she never thought to talk with her pastor and did not know how to pray for her situation.

"Yet I am always with you; you hold me by my right hand."
Psalm 73:23 (NIV)

Unfortunately, the bullying soon escalated into a physical altercation, and in a split second, Josie found herself lying on the floor in the school hallway. Stunned, embarrassed, and afraid, she picked herself up, brushed the dust off her clothes, and headed to class. She tried to ignore the mocking and laughter from the other kids, as she walked away in humiliation. Their words hurt and made her sad. Josie's life was in turmoil as the days progressed. Despite the situation, she had an unexplainable "hope" in her heart. She later came to understand that her persistent hope came from the Lord.

"Now, faith is confidence in what we hope for and assurance about what we do not see." Hebrews 11:1 (NIV)

As a result of the isolation and trauma associated with bullying, Josie never learned how to relax, have fun, or "just be a kid." Despite her hardships, she kept trusting God's promises in the Bible and was confident her Heavenly Father had a plan for her life. As promised, God protected Josie from the adversary's attempts to steal her hope and joy.

"May the God of hope fill you with all joy and peace as you trust in him, so that you may overflow with hope by the power of the Holy Spirit." Romans 15:13 (NIV)

Josie matured into a responsible, loving, and conscientious teen-ager, who cared about others, thanks to the love of her family and God. She babysat her younger sister every day after school, while her classmates enjoyed sports and "hanging out" with their friends. She took her commitments seriously, a trait that followed her into adulthood.

As Josie started high school, her circumstances began to improve. She was grateful when the constant bullying and ridicule transitioned to a tolerable level of teasing. Perhaps the transition was due to her classmates maturing, or maybe things changed as her trust in the Lord expanded. Whatever the reason, she was thankful. Friendships still eluded her, but books and stories continued to fill this void, as she adapted to her unique situation. Her eczema was finally under control, and her self-confidence slowly began to improve.

As time passed, Josie was able to concentrate on her academics without the constant fear of ridicule. Realizing and accepting she would never "easily fit in" to social or school settings, she decided to focus her energy on schoolwork to gain credibility. She felt God's presence in her life as she set her sights on graduating and potentially attending college.

> *"I can do all this through him who gives me strength."*
> *Philippians 4:13 (NIV)*

Despite the odds, Josie graduated from high school and attended a small Christian college in the northeast. Her time in college yielded a Bachelor's degree, some lasting friendships, and an introduction to her future husband. To Josie's surprise, God blessed her with a man who embraced her inquisitive nature and realistic views on life. He became her best friend.

> *"What, then, shall we say in response to these things?*
> *If God is for us, who can be against us?" Romans 8:31 (NIV)*

Soon after they were married, Josie's husband fulfilled his calling to become a pastor. As a married couple, they strive to focus on God while trusting Him with their lives. God blessed them with two children, a daughter who recently graduated from college with honors, and an autistic son, who is making incredible strides in life. Together, they share God's unconditional love with hurting people. They joyfully embrace opportunities to help people fulfill God's purpose for their lives, despite the challenges they may face.

> *"... In this world, you will have trouble.*
> *But take heart! I have overcome the world."*
> *John 16:33 (NIV)*

In closing, after years of suffering, Josie finally learned to be comfortable with her identity. She is a daughter of God, and He loves her unconditionally. He made her for a specific purpose and is in control. While the scars from the past are with her, Josie no longer allows the bullying she endured to define her. She keeps moving forward with her life, and recently received her master's degree, graduating with honors.

Josie shared, "God does not waste any of our experiences, whether good or bad. What the adversary meant for evil in my life, God leveraged and transformed. Based on my experiences, He blessed me with a unique awareness and compassion to support and empathize with my autistic son, in ways I never thought were possible. I keep looking up, holding on to God's promises, and trusting His plan for my life. For if God is for me, who can be against me?"

> *"You intended to harm me, but God intended it for good*
> *to accomplish what is now being done,*
> *the saving of many lives." Genesis 50:20 (NIV)*

REFLECTION

Our Heavenly Father does NOT approve of bullying or harassment. He does not want any of His children to feel unworthy, minimized, or "not good enough." Unfortunately, in this fallen world, Satan uses any means available to steal joy, kill self-esteem, and destroy hope.

> *"The thief comes only to steal and kill and destroy…"*
> *John 10:10 (NIV)*

Bullying can occur at home, school, work, in neighborhoods, with friends, in families, and on sports teams. If you are the victim of bullying (now or in the past), below are some insights from the Bible to help you heal. When you trust God and embrace His promises, He will fill you with love, peace, strength, and joy as you move forward.

You are a child of God.	Galatians 3:26; 2 Corinthians 6:18
You are wonderfully made.	Psalm 139:13-14; Genesis 1:27
You are unique.	Isaiah 64:8; Psalm 119:73
You are valued.	Matthew 6:26; Matthew 10:29-31
You are here for a reason.	Jeremiah 29:11; Romans 8:28
You are strong.	Philippians 4:13; Isaiah 41:10; Isaiah 40:31
You can make a difference.	Philippians 1:6; Matthew 28:19-20
You are loved.	John 3:16; Ephesians 2:8

NEXT STEPS

Words and actions matter. Bullying can be verbal, in writing, emotional, physical, or via the internet (e.g., Facebook, Twitter, Instagram). If you, your child, a family member, a friend, or co-worker are a victim of bullying or harassment, there are several resources available to provide help:

- For the office environment, contact your manager, human resources department, ethics officer, or call your company's 800 hot-line number.

- For bullying at school or cyberbullying, you can reach out to the student's teacher, bus driver, school counselor, or principal.

- Your local police department, minister, pastor, priest, or counselor can also provide guidance and assistance to stop bullying.

- The U.S official website to "stop bullying": https://www.stopbullying.gov/

CLOSING PRAYER

Dear Heavenly Father,

My heart breaks when I think about the children and adults in this world who endure the painful effects of bullying and harassment. It leaves emotional scars, which can last a lifetime. If I ever see or hear someone being bullied or harassed, please give me the courage and strength to help that person in their time of need. I love you. Amen.

A Restored Marriage

It was a Friday evening before a long holiday weekend. Sandy and Sean were still at the office, finishing up some business discussions. One thing led to another, and they lost track of time as they laughed and enjoyed each other's company. Then, Sandy casually said, "Hey, my husband and daughter are out of town this weekend. Since you are by yourself, do you want to grab dinner?" Without hesitating, Sean said yes.

Sandy's beginnings were happy and down-to-earth. She was born in a small town where neighbors cared for neighbors, and life centered around family, community, and church activities. God blessed her with loving, kind, and caring parents, plus a devoted extended family. Her father was an electrician for the local school district, while her Mom stayed home to raise Sandy and her younger sister.

Despite their modest family income, Sandy's mother had aspirations to appear as if they were part of a "higher class." She was a sharp dresser, and the girls wore beautiful clothing. When Sandy was eight, her father accepted a senior electrician position in a town an hour away. A few months after they moved, her mother started a part-time job, since the girls were getting older.

Eventually, Sandy's mother started to work full time to help cover the bills, as her persistent desire to be part of a higher class continued. Sadly, her mother's drive to appear as if they had money, began to impact how Sandy viewed herself. She started to think, "I'm am not good enough," a feeling and belief that followed her for many years.

"If anyone thinks they are something when they are not,
they deceive themselves." Galatians 6:3 (NIV)

As life continued, Sandy grew into a beautiful and vibrant woman on the outside, but on the inside, she lacked self-confidence and believed she was never enough. She graduated from college and landed some impressive jobs in New York City. Despite her outward appearance, Sandy silently struggled with self-esteem challenges and never seemed to be satisfied. She occasionally attended church but did not have a "personal relationship" with God.

"But seek first his kingdom and his righteousness..."
Matthew 6:33 (NIV)

Sandy jumped from relationship to relationship searching for a big, strong man who would make her feel validated and complete, but no one was able to fill the hole in her heart. Unfortunately, she was attracted to powerful, upper-class men with strong and prominent personalities, on the spectrum of narcissists. Men who kept her on edge as they fed their egos and played mind games to the detriment of her self-esteem. Sandy was caught in a vicious cycle and felt unworthy of love. She relied on men to validate her self-worth versus looking to God.

"For where you have envy and selfish ambition,
there you find disorder and every evil practice."
James 3:16 (NIV)

By the time Sandy was in her late twenties, the majority of her friends were married or engaged. She was embarrassed that no one wanted to marry her and thought, "Why am I not good enough. What's wrong with me?" Her self-confidence hit a new low, as love and contentment continued to elude her.

Despite her inner turmoil and sadness, she maintained her outward façade, pretending life was great. But silently, Sandy realized something was wrong with her perspective on life. She began to ponder what was next for her, and wondered if this was all life had to offer?

In her silent despair, Sandy allowed herself to take an honest look at her life. She recalled growing up and enjoying a close relationship with God, and realized she missed her Heavenly Father. Due to her preoccupation with "trying to be good enough" as measured by earthly goals, she had turned her back on God and ignored Him.

"Do not conform to the pattern of this world,
but be transformed by the renewing of your mind..."
Romans 12:2 (NIV)

Sandy began a deep, soul searching journey as she started to reread the Bible, attend church, and pray. She was keenly aware that life on her own, separated from God, was not working. Sandy was tired of being sad and lonely, relying on men to fill the void in her heart. She needed to stop worshiping men and start worshiping her Heavenly Father.

"The Lord is near to all who call on him,
to all who call on him in truth." Psalm 145:18 (NIV)

Finally, Sandy chose to be completely transparent with God. She prayed and cried as she openly shared her heartbreaks, mistakes, and fears with her Heavenly Father. She admitted failing to follow His commandments and asked for forgiveness. Sandy wanted to pursue a new life centered around a relationship with Jesus as her personal Savior, without the baggage from her past life. God lovingly embraced her at that moment, just the way she was.

"Repent, then, and turn to God, so that your sins
may be wiped out, that times of refreshing
may come from the Lord." Acts 3:19 (NIV)

For the next several years, love, commitment, and marriage continued to elude Sandy as she faithfully asked God to bless her with a Christian husband. She continued to trust God and wait on His timing.

Then, a surprising thing happened. Sandy entered into a relationship with a Christian friend she had known for nearly five years.

> *"But those who hope in the Lord will renew their strength.*
> *They will soar on wings like eagles;*
> *they will run and not grow weary,*
> *they will walk and not be faint." Isaiah 40:31 (NIV)*

Steve was unlike any man she previously dated. He was patient, kind, and tried to put her feelings first. After a short engagement, they became husband and wife. Steve and Sandy decided to start a family right away since she was now in her late thirties, and her biological clock was ticking.

Unfortunately, Sandy faced infertility challenges, and they suffered through several miscarriages. The heartbreaks placed a strain on their marriage. Finally, after three long years, God blessed them with a sweet little girl. They were thrilled and praised God for their daughter.

> *"He settles the childless woman in her home*
> *as a happy mother of children. Praise the Lord."*
> *Psalm 113:9 (NIV)*

Sandy desired to be a stay-at-home Mom, but due to financial constraints, she reluctantly returned to work. She wanted Steve to work harder and provide a better income for their family, but he was not an overly ambitious man. His priorities were different compared to the men Sandy dated previously in her life. During this time, fractures began to surface in their marriage due to their different aspirations in life.

Regrettably, the unaddressed fractures in their marriage grew into anger and resentment. Communication became a significant issue, and they spent a great deal of their time arguing. They had difficulty reaching "common ground" on most things, and there was constant friction regarding parenting approaches. To complicate the situation, their daughter had some health challenges, which placed an additional strain on their marriage.

*"Above all, love each other deeply, because love covers
over a multitude of sins." 1 Peter 4:8 (NIV)*

While they continued to attend church together, it became more of a façade than a way of life. Sandy was preoccupied with worldly things and "stressed-out" as she tried to balance an unfulfilling job, handle her daughter's health issues, be a wife, and take care of their home. She was exhausted and began to smoke cigarettes as a way to cope. Steve was doing his best to run his own business, but the company did not grow as they hoped.

*"Do not be anxious about anything, but in every situation,
by prayer and petition, with thanksgiving,
present your requests to God." Philippians 4:6 (NIV)*

When school bullying issues began to surface, Sandy once again emphasized her desire to quit work and be available when their daughter came home from school each day. She was frustrated with Steve and believed he was "not stepping up" to financially support his family. Disappointment and feelings of bitterness placed further pressures on their relationship.

As Steve and Sandy entered their fifteenth year of marriage, they transferred their daughter to a private school to remove her from the persistent bullying. Around this same time, her health challenges began to stabilize, and they were finally able to relax. But regrettably, their marriage was on rocky ground, and there was no clear path for restoration.

As time passed, Sandy continued to work to help meet their financial obligations. Reluctantly, she landed a new job working with an executive leadership team at a Fortune 500 company. Once again, Sandy found herself surrounded by powerful, successful men — an environment she knew very well.

Sandy's new job was challenging, but one Division President named Sean caught her eye from the very beginning. She admired his work ethic, technical expertise, and the way he interacted with her. She also noticed he was strong, handsome, powerfully built, and going through a divorce. They kindled a positive working relationship, a relationship that transitioned into a special friendship.

Unfortunately, Satan was not through with Sandy. He knew her weaknesses regarding strong men and began to tempt her in small ways, assuring her, it was okay. At first, her interactions with Sean included harmless joking and casual conversations, but it soon grew into flirting and looking for reasons to spend time with him. Satan's temptations expanded as Sandy turned her focus away from God and toward her human desire to have a powerful man here on earth.

> *"Watch and pray so that you will not fall into temptation.*
> *The spirit is willing, but the flesh is weak."*
> *Matthew 26:41 (NIV)*

Then one Friday evening, Sandy and Sean were still at the office, finishing up some business discussions. One thing led to another, and they lost track of time as they laughed and enjoyed each other's company. Then, Sandy casually said, "Hey, my husband and daughter are out of town this weekend. Since you are by yourself, do you want to grab dinner?" Without hesitating, Sean said yes.

> *"...but each person is tempted when they are*
> *dragged away by their own evil desire and enticed."*
> *James 1:14 (NIV)*

Instead of grabbing dinner by the office, they drove in separate cars to an exclusive restaurant about twenty minutes away. It was very romantic. Sandy was captivated the entire evening as she enjoyed the company of this handsome, strong, and successful man. She loved being the center of his attention and felt special.

> *"Be alert and of sober mind.*
> *Your enemy, the devil, prowls around*
> *like a roaring lion looking for someone to devour."*
> *1 Peter 5:8 (NIV)*

As the evening came to a close, Sean walked Sandy to her car. An unexpected, passionate kiss led to a hotel room, and that night, Satan had Sandy exactly where he wanted her. It was the beginning of secret rendezvous and encounters that were in defiance of her Christian and moral beliefs.

"You shall not commit adultery." Exodus 20:14 (NIV)

Sandy knew her affair was wrong, but she became trapped in her sins of adultery, lust, and worldly satisfaction. She shared, "I chose to ignore God as I focused on my extramarital affair. It was the only way I could do it. God would have kept me from pursuing the relationship I desperately wanted. I didn't want God to stop me." Sean temporally filled the hole in her heart, and she idolized him.

"So I say, walk by the Spirit,
and you will not gratify the desires of the flesh."
Galatians 5:16 (NIV)

Sandy continued to live with her husband, but her focus and positive energy were devoted to Sean and her daughter. Their marriage was in shambles. Before long, her husband moved into the basement as they contemplated a formal separation and divorce.

Sandy no longer loved her husband and hated to be around him. She resented him for failing to be a strong man that she could idolize and worship. But Steve was unwilling to give up on their marriage and began to pray. He begged God to restore their marriage.

As the affair continued, a remarkable thing began to unfold in Sandy's life. While her husband faithfully prayed for his family and marriage, God surrounded her with four strong Christian women from different areas in her life. These women began to pray for her relationship with God and her marriage. Sandy was amazed and realized this was not a coincidence.

As the months passed, an interesting phenomenon transpired. Slowly, God began to transform Sandy's "stone heart." She started to take prayer walks in the evening, so she could pray and talk with God. Before long, she began taking "deep discussion walks" early each morning with her husband. God was with her on every walk. Her Heavenly Father never left or abandoned her during the affair or her betrayal, even though she turned her back on Him. Yes, Sandy exercised her free will, but God still loved her.

Then one day, Sandy was overwhelmed with guilt, and she openly confessed her sins to a priest. She shared, "I was afraid I was going to burn in hell if I did not change what I was doing." But Satan still had a hold on her. Sandy fell in love with Sean, and she saw him as the keys to her happiness. She didn't want to settle but also knew her affair was wrong.

Hebrews 10:26-27 (NIV)

If we deliberately keep on sinning
after we have received the
knowledge of the truth,
no sacrifice for sins is left,
but only a fearful expectation of judgment
and of raging fire that will
consume the enemies of God.

Steve finally found an apartment and made preparations to move out of the basement. Before he moved out, he asked Sandy to go to their church and pray with him one last time. As they were on their knees, she silently prayed to God and said, "If I ask Steve not to move out, I will lose my happiness. Help me to let him go or to stop him from moving out." Suddenly, Sandy turned to Steve and blurted out, "Don't move out; we can work through this." She then quietly said to God, "There goes my happiness."

Real-life is not always pretty, but there is good news! God is in the business of restoration for individuals and marriages! Sean soon broke off the affair with Sandy, and she knew God was in control and doing what was best for her.

Sandy chose to turn her focus toward God and her marriage. She began to pray for God's guidance. She also agreed to attend counseling in an attempt to put their marriage back together. There were many weeks of tears, and gut-wrenching conversations as Sandy's faithful friends continued to pray.

"Repent, then, and turn to God,
so that your sins may be wiped out,
that times of refreshing may come from the Lord."
Acts 3:19 (NIV)

Then, one day, Sandy fully reopened her heart to God and prayed, "Father, please forgive me. Help me to be a good wife and to love my husband. Please change my heart." Then one evening, she was by herself in her kitchen, quietly having a conversation with God. Suddenly, in her head, she heard her Heavenly Father speak with great kindness. He said, "Sandy, you want a man to worship. You are not going to get that. You are to worship me." She was overwhelmed with clarity and gratitude.

"If we confess our sins, he is faithful and just
and will forgive us our sins...." 1 John 1:9 (NIV)

Before long, Sandy and Steve started to pray together. They conscientiously placed God in the center of their marriage, and as a couple, began to grow in their faith. They continued their morning walks, holding hands as they listened and talked. After several months, Sandy started to see Steve through the eyes of Jesus, and God restored their love.

They are now partners, as they worship, pray, and enjoy a happy life as husband and wife. Their daughter experienced some rough patches in her late teens, so together, they sought God's guidance and direction. They now help and encourage each other on their journey.

Sandy shared, "I knowingly sinned and turned away from God and my husband. I was wrong, and I am so very sorry. But thankfully, through the amazing grace of Jesus, I was forgiven, and my sins were wiped away. God's love and grace opened a new door for my spirituality and life. He restored me, and then my marriage. I am so grateful."

"...as far as the east is from the west,
so far has he removed our transgressions from us."
Psalm 103:12 (NIV)

She continued, "Steve and I now enjoy a deep love and affection for each other. I finally understand what true love looks like."

---

1 Corinthians 13:4-8 (NIV)

Love is patient, love is kind.
It does not envy, it does not boast,
it is not proud. It does not dishonor others,
it is not self-seeking, it is not easily angered,
it keeps no record of wrongs.
Love does not delight in evil
but rejoices with the truth.
It always protects, always trusts,
always hopes, always perseveres.

In closing, Sandy said, "My story is raw and truthful. My pride and human desires nearly destroyed our marriage and me. Thankfully, I am now a better person because of the grace of God. If you are experiencing marital problems, please ask God to intervene and fight for your marriage. God is so faithful. Thankfully, I am now looking forward to growing old with my best friend."

"For all have sinned and fall short of the glory of God."
Romans 3:23 (NIV)

REFLECTION

Fractured relationships are painful and exhausting — but there is good news! God can and will restore broken relations in your life, whether it be your marriage, conflicts with family members, or friendships that slipped away.

1. Pause and Reflect. Do you have a broken relationship in your life? What happened?

   _____

   _____

   _____

   _____

   _____

   _____

2. Secret and embarrassing relationships not only affect you but negatively impact the people around you. Is there a relationship you are attempting to hide from your family, friends, spouse, or God?

   _____

   _____

   _____

   _____

   If you answered yes, pause for a moment. Be honest with yourself and God. Why are you trying to hide the relationship?

   _____

   _____

   _____

NEXT STEPS

Satan takes advantage of our weaknesses when we turn away from God. He strives to keep us separated from the light of God's love by making us feel unworthy. Thankfully, there is good news! Regardless of our past, if we confess our sins and ask for forgiveness, God erases our sins as we strive to do what is right in the eyes of the Lord.

> *"Come now, let us settle the matter," says the Lord.*
> *"Though your sins are like scarlet,*
> *they shall be as white as snow;*
> *though they are red as crimson,*
> *they shall be like wool."*
> *Isaiah 1:18 (NIV)*

Do you want to take steps to restore a relationship? Do you need to stop pursuing a relationship that is hurting you and your family? Take the steps below to begin your restoration journey.

- Stop hiding! God already sees everything in your life. He sees all your actions and hears every thought in your head. He knows your heart. Turn the relationship over to God and ask Him for help.
- If you feel trapped in sin and do not know how to get out, ask God to help you. He loves you and is waiting to listen.
- Pray the prayer below.

CLOSING PRAYER

Dear God,

My heart is hurting. I made some mistakes and need your help to restore my relationship with _____. Please forgive me for _____. Guide and direct me on the next steps I need to take. I love you. Amen.

Our Journey as
Foster Care Parents

"Whoever welcomes one of these little children
in my name welcomes me; and whoever welcomes me
does not welcome me but the one who sent me."
Mark 9:37 (NIV)

Kate was exhausted, and bedtime was once again a challenge. She finally tucked her little foster child into bed, then took a deep breath. Their nighttime routine was not over. Together, they read a short story, then said their goodnight prayers. As Kate quietly walked across the room to turn out the lights, this sweet little child softly said, "Please tell Jesus not to forget me."

We never know the paths our lives will take, but we do know that with God, all things are possible. Mike and Kate had recently celebrated their fifteenth wedding anniversary and were enjoying their children, ages ten, eight, and four. Mike was a county police officer, and Kate transitioned from a full-time social worker to a stay-at-home mom. Their family worshipped together, played together, and truly enjoyed being with each other. Life was great!

"For with God, nothing shall be impossible."
Luke 1:37 (KJV)

Despite their happy life, the kids frequently shared how much they wanted a younger brother or sister. It was a topic that never seemed to go away. Kate's biological clock was ticking, so pursuing another pregnancy was not an option they wanted to explore. Before long, they started to research the steps involved with adopting a baby. During this time, Mike suggested they look into foster care. Together, they began to pray for God's guidance and direction.

Through websites and research, they learned that foster care parents provide a loving, temporary home for a child who is in an unsafe or risky situation due to neglect, abuse, or other circumstances. It's a big responsibility. While the child is in a foster home, the local county seeks to address any medical or unique support requirements the child may have. They also deal with the issues that caused the county to remove the child from their family home.

The goal of social workers and the county is to have the foster child safely return to their home with their parent or parents. When this goal is not possible, the county and social workers make alternative plans to identify a safe and nurturing home environment for the child. In some cases, the alternate approach might include living with grandparents or adoption.

As the weeks passed, Mike and Kate continued to pray as they seriously considered foster care parenting. They had discussions with their pastor, who openly shared his experiences going through the foster care program as a child, and the positive impact it had on his life. They also spoke with foster parents regarding the challenges, obstacles, and rewards of embarking on this new lifestyle. Finally, they candidly discussed foster care with their children, since having additional kids in their home would touch every member of their family. All three kids were excited to help other children.

The thought of becoming foster parents was scary, and there were many unknowns, so they kept trusting God and asked for clarity regarding their next steps. After weeks of prayer and soul searching, Mike and Kate both knew it was the right time to open their home to a young boy or girl who needed their love, help, and support. So, they stepped out in faith and formally began the lengthy and detailed process to become foster parents.

Kate shared, "As we embarked on our foster care journey, we were nervous, and there were many unknowns, but we wanted to be obedient to God's will for our lives. We viewed foster care as an opportunity to be the hands and feet of Jesus here on earth — to care for little children in need. We also realized we would have many partners on our journey, including social workers, doctors, lawyers, schools, and community resources to help us meet the children's needs."

The verification, approval, and licensing process to become foster care parents took several weeks. Some of the requirements included:

Mandatory Training — To ensure they understood the county's foster care processes, procedures, and required reporting. The training occurred over three consecutive Saturdays and equipped them with parenting skills for children with special needs.

A Family Assessment — To confirm Kate and Mike had the right desire, demeanor, and nurturing abilities to make a difference in the life of a child, plus the time and flexibility to meet the on-going demands of foster parenting. After they completed several detailed questionnaires regarding their personal history and family, the county conducted three separate interviews, including one meeting that took place in their home. This process also helped the county understand which children (e.g., ages, challenges, etc.) would best fit into their family.

Investigations — To validate their financial and emotional stability. Part of this process included reference checks, fingerprinting, protective services, criminal background checks, plus an assessment of their driving and financial records. (Note: Families are provided a small reimbursement stipend to offset the foster child's expenses while they are living in a foster home.)

Home Inspections — To ensure their home met fire/safety regulations and had adequate space for another child.

Verifications — To review their home/auto insurance policies, ensure pets were vaccinated, confirm a home emergency plan was in place, validate their CPR and first aid certifications, and ensure confidentiality statements were signed.

Finally, after months of prayer and preparation, they were approved, licensed, and accepted into the "foster care family." While joy and excitement filled their hearts, they were also anxious and nervous. They might be responsible for children with emotional, behavioral, developmental, or medical needs. Some children may have endured neglect or abuse, while others could be dealing with parents who are in jail or strung-out on drugs. Still, others might need help due to the death of their parents, or families that are struggling as a result of poverty, mental illness, or homelessness.

"Cast all your anxiety on him because he cares for you."
1 Peter 5:7 (NIV)

As they began to pray for the children that God would place in their home, they decided to start their foster care journey with short-term support called "respite." This program allows exhausted foster parents to have a break and re-energize for a few days or a weekend, while another licensed family cares for their foster children. For the next eighteen months, Mike and Kate cared for approximately thirty different children; some stayed with them several different times.

Then, an unforeseen challenge entered their lives. Kate learned she had thyroid cancer. They prayed about her situation, placed her diagnosis in God's hands, then proceeded with the doctor's recommended treatments. They knew God had a plan for their lives as foster care parents, and they were not going to waiver. As she finished her cancer treatments, the county called and asked if they would accept their first full-time foster child. They said yes.

Mike and Kate were on a steep learning curve as a nervous, fifteen-year-old girl moved into their home. Thankfully, after a few days, they came up with routines, and she transitioned nicely into their family. Fortunately, this teenage girl had a happy ending. She had regular visits with her family as the county worked closely with her parents to deal with an unsafe and severe hoarding situation in their home. After four months, and a lot of hard work, the local Fire Marshall declared their house was safe, and she returned home. God answered their prayers.

Kate and Mike continued to pray daily for the children that God would place in their home. Before long, they had the opportunity to care for a sweet three-year-old little girl, and the entire family fell in love with her. They decided to adopt her but soon learned that another loving family had already started the adoption process. They were thrilled she would have a permanent and loving home, but they were also heartbroken.

Shortly after she was adopted, they received a call to take-in a six-year-old girl. Due to their recent feelings of loss, they needed time to re-energize and heal, so they said no. Then, for some reason, every day over the next four months, Kate kept thinking about this little girl that she never met, and she started to pray for her. Then, out of the blue, a county social worker called their home and said, "You know the girl you keep checking on? Well, she needs a home." When Kate heard these words, she began jumping up and down. She knew God had a plan for little Mary to be in their life, and they said yes.

> *"For I know the plans I have for you," declares the Lord, "plans to prosper you and not to harm you, plans to give you hope and a future." Jeremiah 29:11 (NIV)*

Mary's story was heartbreaking. Social services intervened and removed her from an unsafe situation several months earlier. Her alcoholic father sexually abused her, and her mother was verbally abusive. Their hearts ached for her.

Kate, Mike, and the kids lovingly accepted her into their family, and she quickly began to blossom. Mary started to do better in school, was full of questions, and happily attended church with them every Sunday. She wanted to learn about God, despite other adults in her life telling her that He did not exist. During this happy time in her life, social services made sure Mary had regular visits with her mother. They also helped her mom get the counseling and support she needed.

"Learn to do right; seek justice. Defend the oppressed.
Take up the cause of the fatherless..." Isaiah 1:17 (NIV)

Then one night, Kate was exhausted as she tried to get all the kids into bed. When she tucked Mary into her bed, they read a short story, then said their goodnight prayers. As Kate quietly walked across the room to turn out the lights, this sweet little child softly said, "Please tell Jesus not to forget me."

As the months passed, Mary's alcoholic father was no longer in the picture, and her mother's demeanor changed for the better. After months of observations and support, social services determined it was safe for Mary to leave her foster family and move back home with her mother. Just before she left, she shared, "I am so relieved. I knew there was a God, and knew he loved me." They were thankful, and their hearts overflowed.

"...Let the little children come to me, and do not hinder them,
for the kingdom of God belongs to such as these."
Mark 10:14 (NIV)

Mike and Kate were grateful when Mary returned home, yet they were sad and missed her. Thankfully, there is good news! Since she moved only a mile from their home, the families kept in touch. When her mother works, Mary stays with Kate and Mike. They also pick her up for church on Sunday mornings. She has grown into a confident teenager and recently made the middle school honor program. Kate shared, "We are grateful God allows us to watch her life unfold. We look forward to enjoying many happy years with Mary in our lives."

As each foster child left their home, Mike and Kate would pause and have a family meeting with their biological children. They wanted to ensure their children were still comfortable with foster kids living in their home. Every time they had the discussion, their children expressed compassion for the kids who lived with them and were happy they could help them. The entire family was blessed and grateful for the opportunity to make the world a better place, one child at a time.

Shortly after Mary left their home, social services called again. This time, they were asked to care for fifteen-month-old twins. Within three days, their lives drastically changed. They were dealing with bottles and diapers for two severely neglected toddlers. Their parents were on drugs, had arrest records, and their mother was a prostitute. Their little lives were a mess.

Kate and Mike felt ill-equipped for the emotional rollercoaster of raising twins. She shared, "There were so many challenges and issues with the twins due to their parent's drug use and neglect. We were overwhelmed, but we also knew God was with us. There were many sleepless nights when they would scream for hours, and nothing would ease their anxiety. I quickly surrendered the twins to God, as I trusted Him for wisdom, strength, and peace." The following Bible verse carried Kate through many days and nights:

*"When I am afraid, I put my trust in you. In God, whose word
I praise—in God, I trust and am not afraid.
What can mere mortals do to me?" Psalm 56:3-4 (NIV)*

Taking care of the twins' daily needs, such as feeding, bathing, changing diapers, and playtime was just part of their responsibilities. While Mike was at work, Kate would take the twins to appointments with doctors, social workers, and of course, supervised visits with their parents. When she got home, Kate would spend time with her kids and help with homework, fix dinner, do laundry, then get all the kids ready for bed. On some nights, she would pray, "Dear God, please help me put these kids to bed."

*"God is our refuge and strength,
an ever-present help in trouble." Psalm 46:1 (NIV)*

For thirteen months, the twins were an integrated part of their family. During this time, social workers determined their mother was not fit to be in their lives, but it was clear their father and grandparents loved them very much. After a great deal of focus, investigations, and inspections, the county determined the twins could live with their paternal grandparents and father.

Kate and Mike struggled with the transition decision and offered to keep the twins longer, but the county felt this move was in the best interest of the children. The entire family wept when the twins left their home. Kate shared, "It ripped our hearts out when the twins moved away. We love them and pray for them daily."

Within a few months, they accepted a sweet one-year-old boy into their home and embraced this child with love, empathy, and compassion. And a year later, another baby was placed in their home. The stories of the foster care children who have lived with this loving family go on and on. Kate shared, "It is such a gift to see God work in the lives of our foster children. Despite the challenges that each child has, our Heavenly Father somehow strengthens us and gives us the ability to meet the needs of each child."

While caring for full-time foster children, they continued to provide respite services for other foster parents. There was one teenage boy named Ben who stayed with them over many respite weekends. He had a tender heart and cared about others. They worried about him as he moved from foster home to foster home. He seemed to be "falling through the cracks," and his situation tugged on their hearts. They knew it was difficult to place older kids in foster care homes. Finally, Mike and Kate asked the county to assign Ben to their home, so they could provide him with a stable environment. The county agreed.

Due to the events in Ben's life, he was angry, frustrated, and confused. As he prepared to start his senior year in high school, he was facing an uphill challenge to graduate. He could not fail any more classes. Despite his situation, he was committed to work hard and do his best. He wanted to succeed in life and overcome the challenges of his childhood.

With the help of his foster parents, Ben laid out plans to graduate from high school, then enroll in the local community college. It helped to have plans, but he still worried about his future since foster care services change at age eighteen. Mike and Kate regularly reassured him not to worry — he would always have a home with them. Ben's story continues to unfold as his foster parents continue to pray for him.

"Defend the weak and the fatherless;
uphold the cause of the poor and the oppressed."
Psalm 82:3 (NIV)

Mike and Kate shared, "Foster parenting is very challenging, but it is also the most rewarding experience of our lives. It's a privilege to care for the children God places in our home. It provides us with an opportunity to play a small role in the lives of children who unfortunately experienced devastating losses of family, security, and self-worth. These children arrive at our front door, feeling frightened and alone, but we know God has a plan for their lives, and we are grateful for the chance to help and love them."

Kate then shared, "Through our foster care experiences, I have drawn closer to God. He strengthens me to meet the needs of each child and gives me patience when they throw tantrums or "act out their pain" due to their past traumas. I celebrate when the kids take one step forward and pray for them when they are struggling. For you see, our foster children are so much more than their behaviors or horrific stories. They are children of God, and we love them."

"Rescue the weak and the needy; deliver them from
the hand of the wicked." Psalm 82:4 (NIV)

In closing, she said, "We have a window into the children's pain and hurts, as well as the opportunity to watch God at work in their lives. Every night, when I pray for my family and children, I also pray for each foster child, by name, who has lived in our home. I am so grateful God granted us the opportunity to serve Him through foster care parenting. To God, be the Glory! Amen."

REFLECTION

No child should live in fear, brokenness, or darkness. They should never feel as if they are a burden, unworthy, or worthless. No child should see their parents overdose on drugs, or pass out from too much alcohol. They should never be physically, mentally, or verbally abused. No child should feel invisible, or ever think their life does not matter. They should never feel unsafe, unloved, or unwanted.

Pause and Reflect. How can you make a small or big difference in a hurting child's life? What are you willing to do this week or this month to make a difference?

_____

_____

_____

NEXT STEPS

States and counties across America are looking for foster care parents. If you feel God tugging on your heart to explore this type of service to children in need, there are a few steps you can take:

- Pray and ask God for direction.
- Contact the National Foster Parent Association (NFPA), or your local county, for additional information about foster care. https://nfpaonline.org/
- Reach out and help a foster parent in your neighborhood, office, or church this week. Deliver a meal or dessert, or perhaps send an encouraging card/email. Any positive gestures of support will be greatly appreciated.

CLOSING PRAYER

Dear Heavenly Father,

Today, I want to pause and ask you to bless the people who choose to "be in service" through foster care. Please encourage their hearts as you give them wisdom, courage, and patience. Also, I ask for a special blessing for the children in foster care programs, and the young adults who "aged out" and are now on their own. Please light their paths and protect them. Thank you. Amen.

Surviving Domestic Abuse

"The Lord is a refuge for the oppressed,
a stronghold in times of trouble." Psalm 9:9 (NIV)

As his anger and screaming escalated, Doug drove faster and faster. Suddenly, he reached across the car, grabbed Sue's long hair, and jerked her face toward him. Then he hatefully screamed, "I'm talking to you. You better pay attention." At that point, he threw her head against the passenger window and accelerated the car.

Sue was a divorced, single mother raising two little girls in the suburbs of Washington, D.C. She maintained a cordial relationship with her ex-husband, and they shared joint custody of their daughters. Sue balanced her parenting and work responsibilities while ensuring the girls grew up in a Christian home environment. By the time she was thirty-one, she was working full time for a Fortune 500 company and looking forward to a promising career.

Then one day, while at the office, Sue met a company executive who was relocating to Northern Virginia from the west coast. She was immediately captivated by his intelligence, appearance, and charming personality. Doug was sixteen years older, but he was in great shape and worked out regularly. As time passed, Doug eventually invited Sue to a romantic dinner, and they started to date.

Doug was a captivating gentleman, and he quickly swept Sue off her feet. He handled everything with finesse and confidence. She felt like Cinderella as they enjoyed elegant dinners, and he sang to her with his beautiful voice. Everything about their relationship was like a fairytale. Doug never missed an opportunity to make her feel special, and he was terrific with her girls. He professed to be a Christian, and they occasionally attended church together, but it was not a primary focus for their relationship.

"But seek first his kingdom and his righteousness..."
Matthew 6:33 (NIV)

After eight months, Doug proposed and gave Sue a stunning, two-carat diamond ring. She was "caught up" in their fast-moving romance and wanted their future to be great. They continued to live separately, as they made plans to lease a new home for their life together with the girls. Unfortunately, Sue began to see some "red flags" over the next few months, but she was in love and rationalized her concerns away. She wanted the fairy-tale.

One day, shortly after their engagement, Doug was on business travel near his former home. Sue missed him, so she called his hotel room one evening. To her surprise, a woman answered the phone. Sue said, "Oh, I'm sorry. They must have connected me to the wrong room." The woman replied, "Who are you looking for?" Sue responded, "Doug." Then the woman said, "He's not here, but should be back soon." Shocked, she replied, "Oh, OK. Please tell him Sue called."

She was "thrown off" by the phone call, and did not know what to think. A few hours later, Doug called to apologize for missing her call. He went on to explain that the woman who answered the phone was his former girlfriend. He said they had some unresolved things to discuss and assured her there was no reason to be concerned. Sue wanted to believe him, and his excuse seemed plausible, so she decided to drop her "red flag" and move forward. She was in love.

"The Lord detests lying lips, but he delights in people
who are trustworthy." Proverbs 12:22 (NIV)

They married fourteen months after their first date. At their wedding reception, Sue noticed her new husband drinking a large amount of wine, and it concerned her. Throughout their months of dating, she never saw Doug overindulge with alcohol. Sue also felt his behavior toward her was different throughout their entire wedding day — he was the not the charming, kind man who captured her heart. Before the reception was over, he was drunk.

That night, when they went to their honeymoon suite, Doug passed out. Sue remembers thinking, "What have I done? Have I married someone who has a potential drinking problem and is not nice?" It was at this point, Sue's nightmare began.

"Wine is a mocker and beer a brawler;
whoever is led astray by them is not wise."
Proverbs 20:1 (NIV)

The next day, Doug returned to his old, charming self. He never acknowledged being drunk on their wedding night, and Sue avoided the topic. Life moved forward as they resumed their normal work routine and moved into their new home. The girls lived with them part-time and spent the remaining time with their father.

About two months into their marriage, Sue suggested they transition to one health insurance and change the beneficiaries on their life insurance policies. When she suggested this, Doug became very agitated, and it alarmed her. He accused her of trying to "get something out of him." Sue attempted to explain that married couples typically take care of this type of paperwork, but she was unable to rationalize with him, so she dropped the discussion.

"My dear brothers and sisters, take note of this:
Everyone should be quick to listen,
slow to speak, and slow to become angry,
because human anger does not produce
the righteousness that God desires." James 1:19-20 (NIV)

Doug began to pick-up dinner on his way home from work to make life easier for his wife. Sue appreciated his kind gestures but noticed each time Doug brought home dinner — he also picked up two or three bottles of wine. The number of wine bottles bothered her. She also observed he stayed up late after she went to bed, listening to music and drinking. When he would finally come to bed, she could smell alcohol, and he would quickly pass out. The next morning, she would find two or three empty bottles in the trash. Only a few months into their marriage, Sue realized her husband was a functioning alcoholic.

"Do not get drunk on wine, which leads to debauchery.
Instead, be filled with the Spirit."
Ephesians 5:18 (NIV)

As their arguing became a daily routine, Sue had the girls temporarily live with their father on a full-time basis until she could get things "under control." She did not want her girls subjected to the negative environment. It was at this point Sue approached her husband and shared her concerns about his drinking. Sue also suggested they see a marriage counselor about their relationship. She told Doug they were growing apart and unable to have healthy discussions.

"But the fruit of the Spirit is love, joy, peace,
patience, kindness, goodness, faithfulness,
gentleness and self-control." Galatians 5:22-23 (NIV)

Doug was extremely agitated at Sue for her comments and stated, "I do not have a drinking problem. I only drink wine. There is no problem with our relationship." Doug's agitation quickly transitioned to anger. Sue was afraid to say anything else, so she dropped the topic.

Unfortunately, their arguing continued to escalate, as his nightly binge-drinking continued. His verbal assaults became mentally abusive, and Sue began to experience self-esteem issues. She knew about mental and emotional abuse but never thought it could happen to her. Sue's fairy-tale was falling apart. No one knew she was experiencing gut-wrenching and emotional abuse in the privacy of her home.

"Husbands, love your wives and
do not be harsh with them." Colossians 3:19 (NIV)

Despite their problems at home, she was expected to "play the role" and maintain a façade as a happily married newlywed at the office — after all, he was an executive. Sue soon realized her husband had a split personality, and it made her extremely nervous. She was living on eggshells as she tried to keep "peace," but it was exhausting.

Then one evening, they went to dinner to celebrate Doug's birthday. As they traveled to the restaurant, Doug missed the exit. He immediately became agitated, then started screaming at Sue because she allowed him to "miss the turn." She tried to diffuse the situation and calm him down. She apologized for missing the offramp (even though it was not her responsibility to be his guide.) Sue did not want him to be mad at her.

"Fools give full vent to their rage,
but the wise bring calm in the end."
Proverbs 29:11 (NIV)

They finally made it to the restaurant, but Sue was already exhausted from the verbal abuse she endured in the car. Doug immediately ordered a bottle of wine and started to drink. As the evening progressed, he continued to criticize and belittle her. The more he drank, the louder he became, and Sue was embarrassed. At one point, the maître d' came to the table, laid a rose by her fork, and said, "If you need anything, I am here." She was grateful to know he was monitoring the situation.

When dinner arrived, Doug was drunk. His non-stop, loudmouthed bullying continued, and Sue was mortified. His cruel and demeaning words hurt her heart. Finally, she had enough. She pushed her chair back from the table, stood up, and walked out of the restaurant, halfway through her meal. Sue took the escalator down to the parking garage and started walking toward the car. To her surprise, Doug caught up with her, grabbed her by the arm, and turned her around as he yelled, "Don't you ever leave me again in a restaurant. Get in the car now!"

Sue was afraid of her drunk husband, and she did not want to argue. Without thinking through the situation, she opened the car door, sat down, as he sped away. Doug continued to be irrational, and there was no way to calm him down. She feared he would cause an accident due to his aggressive driving. Sue remembers thinking, "If I open the car door, I wonder if I can jump out without killing myself." As he continued to rant and scream, she did her best to keep quiet and stare out the passenger window.

Then without warning, he reached across the car, grabbed Sue's long hair, and jerked her face toward him. Then he hatefully screamed, "I'm talking to you. You better pay attention." At that point, he threw her head against the window and accelerated the car. Her head throbbed as her heart pounded; she feared they were going to die.

When they arrived home, Doug pulled into the garage and got out of the car. Sue quickly got into the driver's seat but did not have a chance to close the car door. He turned around and said, "Where are you going?" Sue replied, "I'm leaving. I'm leaving you."

Suddenly, in a fit of rage, he grabbed Sue and yanked her out of the car, then physically pulled her up the stairs. Sue tried to fight back as her body hit against the stairs and wall, but he was strong, and she could not break free. He threw her into the master bathroom, then in a fit of rage, began to beat and pummel her as she helplessly laid on the floor.

Sue shared, "Everything seemed to be in slow motion as if I was out-side my body and watching the situation unfold. I was in shock. The pain was excruciating as he continued to hit my face, chest, and back. I just wanted to survive and prayed for God to help me. I did not fight back because he was drunk and bigger than me. I feared any resis-tance could make the situation worse and prolong the beating. I now realize my wisdom "at that moment" came from God.

Suddenly, like a light switch, Doug pulled back and stopped beating her. He then said, "Oh, I'm so sorry — I didn't mean to hurt you. I would never do that, and I will never hit you again." He then tried to hold her bloody and bruised body as she laid on the bathroom floor. He transformed into a different person. A moment later, Sue gained enough strength from an adrenaline rush, to pull herself off the floor and make her way down to the kitchen. She wanted to get away from her husband.

Despite her pain and fear, Sue had clarity and realized she had to make a change. She shared, "My beating was a wake-up call. I knew I could not live in an abusive marriage. I had children and would not subject them to Doug's anger and rage." With newly found courage, she con-fronted her husband and said, "You will never touch me again, or I will report you to the senior officers of the company." He responded, "But I didn't mean to do any of this." She looked at him and stated, "We are getting a divorce."

After they exchanged words, she quietly pulled herself up the stairs, went into a spare bedroom, locked the door, and moved a chest in front of the door. As she crawled into bed, she asked God to keep her safe throughout the night. She was exhausted, and her body throbbed from the brutal beating. In retrospect, Sue realized that confronting her husband, without the aid of others, could have led to her death. She shared, "I know God placed a shield of protection around me that night."

> *"When I am afraid, I put my trust in you. In God, whose*
> *word I praise—in God, I trust and am not afraid.*
> *What can mere mortals do to me?" Psalm 56:3-4 (NIV)*

The next morning, once Sue was confident her husband left for work, she slowly got out of bed and made her way to the mirror. She was shocked to see her battered face but was grateful to be alive. Sue decided not to file a report with the police — she did not want to face the questions or humiliation at work. Instead, she called her best friend, who took pictures of her injured body. Two days later, Sue filed for divorce. She wanted nothing out of the marriage, except her freedom.

Doug moved into an apartment, and Sue remained in the house until the lease ended. Her daughters moved home as she began to pull her life back together. No one knew about the beating, except her best friend and attorney. Sue was a private person and did not want to deal with additional inquiries, speculations, and rumors. She was exhausted and emotionally drained.

Within days of their break-up, Doug began to leave notes on her desk at work and call to say he was watching her. He stalked Sue, and it was creepy. On several occasions, he begged for a second chance, but she asked God for the strength to move forward with the divorce, and God was faithful. She refused to place her life or the girl's lives in jeopardy.

Sue knew her Heavenly Father did not like divorce, but she also realized He did not want one of his daughters to be in an abusive marriage. She was in a fragile state as she moved forward, but continued to trust God completely. Sue was confident He had a plan and purpose for her life. After fourteen months of marriage, the divorce was final, and she was free.

> *"For I know the plans I have for you," declares the Lord,*
> *"plans to prosper you and not to harm you,*
> *plans to give you hope and a future." Jeremiah 29:11 (NIV)*

As time passed, Sue continued to focus on her relationship with God, raise her girls, and build her career. She would occasionally see Doug at the office, but he eventually moved back to the west coast, and she was grateful. Sue later decided to sell her two-carat diamond ring and went to a jeweler to get an appraisal. She was shocked to learn her diamond ring was cubic zirconia. She shared, "It was the perfect end to a perfectly fake relationship."

After seven years passed, an unexpected event unfolded. A man she had known for over ten years invited her to dinner. Robert loved the Lord, and they had many things in common. He had a kind, gentle heart, and genuinely cared about others. They both wanted a Christ-centered marriage, built on mutual respect and love. Before long, they fell in love and were married.

Sue and Robert recently celebrated twenty-five years together and renewed their marriage vows. While there have been some ups and downs over the years, God has abundantly blessed their time together. Her girls are now happily married, and Sue is enjoying many grandchildren.

In closing, Sue shared, "If you find yourself in a verbal, emotional, or physically abusive situation, place your trust in God as you safely seek help. Do not be embarrassed. Abuse is not your fault and, as I discovered, escalates over time. Remember, your abuser is usually remorseful after they attack. Be careful to not fall into false overtures or promises. Pray for strength and courage, and remember God is with you, as you bravely take your next step forward."

REFLECTION

God does not want anyone to be a victim of mental, emotional, or physical abuse. If you are currently living in an abusive relationship or are experiencing the effects of flashbacks due to a prior situation, reach out and get help. Tell a family member, friend, pastor, boss, police officer, or counselor.

- If you are in immediate danger, call 911.
- The 24/7 National Domestic Violence Hotline is 1-800-799-7233.
- Remember, God loves you. You are not alone!

   Pause and Reflect. Are you afraid or embarrassed about something in your life? If you answered yes, are you seeking help, or are you attempting to handle the situation by yourself? Have you asked God for His guidance and peace?

NEXT STEPS

When we invite God into our life, including our painful circumstances, He will provide strength and comfort. God will shine light into our darkness as he guides our way forward.

"The light shines in the darkness,
and the darkness has not overcome it." John 1:5 (NIV)

Is there a painful or embarrassing area in your life that you want to turn over to God? If yes, you can pray the prayer below.

CLOSING PRAYER

Dear Heavenly Father,

You know my situation, even the things that are painful and embarrassing. I can no longer carry this burden alone, and I am releasing it to you right now. Please strengthen me, give me wisdom, and guide my path forward. I love you. Amen.

Raising a Child
with Special Needs

"And we know that in all things God works for the good
of those who love him, who have been
called according to his purpose." Romans 8:28 (NIV)

Indescribable love filled Jenny's heart, as tears of joy ran down her face. After six long years of doctors, hospitals, therapists, and prayers, Nathan finally said her name, "Mommy."

As Mark and Jenny celebrated their first wedding anniversary, they felt it was the right time to start a family. They were in love, had great jobs, and wanted to become parents. Unfortunately, as the months and years passed, Jenny was still not pregnant, and her biological clock was ticking. It was emotionally exhausting and heartbreaking as they tried a variety of fertility treatments, but nothing worked. Finally, after four long years of praying, they decided to pursue "in vitro fertilization" (IVF).

"For I know the plans I have for you," declares the Lord,
"plans to prosper you and not to harm you,
plans to give you hope and a future." Jeremiah 29:11 (NIV)

Friends and family prayed for Jenny and Mark when they embarked on their IVF journey. As a symbol of her faith, at age 34, Jenny placed a prayer for her future child in a "prayer box locket," and vowed never to take it off her neck, until she held their baby in her arms. Thankfully, they soon received exciting news — Jenny was pregnant.

Jenny's Prayer Box Locket

Nearly nine months later, after a perfect pregnancy, doctors delivered their baby boy named Nathan. What should have been a joyous celebration, was clouded when the doctors whisked their new baby away, due to a fever. Unfortunately, this was just the beginning of their challenges. Little Nathan began having seizures and spent the next two weeks in the pediatric intensive care unit (PICU) as the doctors worked to stabilize his condition. Mark and Jenny leaned on God as they feared their baby might die.

It was a particularly hard time for Jenny — it was not supposed to be like this. She wanted the fairy-tale. Instead of enjoying a happy homecoming with their new baby, she was heartbroken and worried. They were not allowed to spend the night in the intensive care unit, and it was gut-wrenching every time she left Nathan. To make the situation worse, Jenny started to doubt herself, and felt as if she was "damaged goods." First, she was not able to get pregnant, and now her baby was struggling. She wondered why this happened. What did she do to deserve this situation? What had she done wrong?

Jenny shared her feelings with her good friend, Terri, a faithful Christian. Terri said, "Jenny, look how many people Nathan has touched in his short life. We don't know what God's plans are for him. Before he was even born, God may have said, 'Nathan, will you do this for me?' Terri's words profoundly changed Jenny's perspective. "This is not about me," she realized.

Finally, despite numerous medications to control his seizures, Nathan was released from the hospital, and they began to settle down into a family routine. Yet as time passed, Jenny realized their baby was missing key developmental milestones. At first, he did not make many sounds and had difficulty holding things in his little hands. As the months passed, he was unable to walk or talk.

As she was dealing with these challenges, Jenny learned she was pregnant with twins. As her tummy grew, so did her anxiety and concerns about Nathan. The situation was overwhelming.

When Nathan turned two, Jenny delivered healthy twin boys, each weighing over seven pounds. They came home from the hospital on Christmas day. Joy and love filled their home. They were now a family of five, with three children in diapers.

As they settled into their expanded parenting roles, Nathan continued to fall further and further behind, when compared to standard developmental milestones. He was unable to walk or speak. Based on his challenges, the county accepted him into their "Child Find Program," an early intervention approach for children with special needs. Mark and Jenny were grateful for the support. They also hired an occupational therapist to work with him several times a week.

Thankfully, when Nathan was two years old, they had a breakthrough. He took his first steps, and they celebrated. However, walking was just the first hurdle that Nathan was facing. Due to his inability to speak, he was extremely frustrated when he tried to express himself and would "act out" by throwing lengthy tantrums. Little Nathan was trapped in his own body and unable to express himself. Jenny and Mark were exhausted and concerned as they prayed for help and clarity.

"Pray continually, give thanks in all circumstances..."
1 Thessalonians 5:17-18 (NIV)

Before long, Nathan began speech therapy. Despite his inability to speak, he learned a few words in sign language. As the months progressed, Nathan and his family learned to sign over two-hundred words. This communication gift removed some of Nathan's anxiety and allowed him to interact with others on a limited basis. It began to "open up" his world, even though he could not talk.

Jenny and Mark had no choice but to work outside their home to make ends meet. It was hard to balance their parent and work responsibilities while also transporting Nathan to doctor, thera-pist, and specialist appointments every week. Thankfully, God gave them the strength and endurance to push forward, and still find joy and peace in the middle of their storm. They loved their three boys and were grateful.

When the twins turned two, they were meeting and exceeding all the developmental milestones. Jenny shared, "There was a stark difference between the twins and four-year-old Nathan. The twins were walking, talking, and playing while Nathan remained trapped inside his little head, and his motor skills were limited. He was still in diapers. We purposely engaged Nathan numerous times a day, as we strived to reach him. While I was thrilled to watch our twins develop and grow at a rapid rate, my heart broke for Nathan. It was devastating."

That same year, Nathan's behavior rapidly deteriorated. His frus-trations continued to intensify from being "locked up in silence" and unable to express himself. About the time Jenny and Mark were at the end of their rope, answers began to emerge regarding Nathan's situation. They learned he had a rare neurological speech disorder called Childhood Apraxia of Speech (CAS).

Jenny shared, "When we researched all the aspects of CAS and understood the severity of his speech disorder, we were terrified. In conjunction with his diagnosis, we realized he was facing other challenges. We continued to pray for Nathan, and on the tough days, we prayed for him several times a day."

It was at this point, his speech therapist made an alarming state-ment to Jenny and Mark, "Nathan will never talk." They were shocked that a professional gave up so quickly on their little boy. They immediately found another therapist and kept moving forward. They were not giving up on their son. They knew God had a purpose for his life.

Each night as they put Nathan to bed, they would pray this prayer with him, "Dear God, please help me talk with my mouth." When they prayed, little Nathan would touch his mouth. At one point, Jenny met with her priest and told him, "I don't know how to pray for my son." Her priest shared, "In the Bible, Jesus shows us that we can ask our Heavenly Father for anything. Based on his example, you can certainly ask God to heal your son."

> *"...he fell with his face to the ground and prayed,*
> *'My Father, if it is possible, may this cup be taken from me.*
> *Yet not as I will, but as you will.'" Matthew 26:39 (NIV)*

Then it happened, Nathan started babbling a few words. They celebrated as each new mumbled word left his lips. Before long, some additional encouragement came their way. Since Nathan had been seizure-free for three years, they were able to stop some of his medications with no negative implications. They thanked God.

As the months progressed, Nathan's vocabulary expanded to about seventy-five words. His words were difficult to understand, and he still struggled to say his name. But, baby step by baby step, Nathan was progressing. He learned how to use a speech app on his iPad, in conjunction with words, as his new speech therapist did everything possible to help ease his frustrations.

Despite his progress, Nathan's aggravations from being imprisoned in his mind continued to intensify. Due to his impulsive behaviors, someone had to watch him 24/7, so he did not accidentally harm himself. To complicate the situation, Nathan was unable to remember rules and did not understand the consequences of not following directions. The only time Jenny and Mark let their guard down was when Nathan slept. They were exhausted.

Jenny shared, "On really tough days, I prayed and focused on God's purpose for Nathan's life. While his behavior was offensive to some, I embraced the fact that he is an innocent little boy with learning disabilities, and God loves him. He has no ego or lofty dreams. He 'lives in the moment' and loves everyone unconditionally."

Amid their stress, God allowed them to have moments with their three children that took their breath away. Their home was full of love. While Nathan could not verbally express how he felt, he shared his feelings through sweet smiles, hugs, and kisses.

She went on to say, "Having a special needs child places unplanned pressure on your marriage. Fortunately, God blessed me with an amazing and compassionate husband. Mark has been a constant source of strength, love, and encouragement. I'm so grateful he is on this journey with me. Together, we do our best to support each other while striving to be loving parents for our three children. Despite Nathan's tough situation, we continue to place our faith and trust in God as we maneuver through this unknown territory."

> *"I have told you these things,*
> *so that in me you may have peace.*
> *In this world you will have trouble. But take heart!*
> *I have overcome the world." John 16:33 (NIV)*

As Nathan's story continued to unfold, his little brothers showed empathy and compassion that was amazing to watch. They helped their big brother get on his shoes, find his favorite balls when he was upset, and hold his hand whenever they left their house. They didn't judge Nathan or make fun of him. They weren't embarrassed or concerned regarding what people thought about their big brother. They were proud of Nathan. At age four, the twins exhibited God's unconditional love and compassion for a little boy who needed help.

Then after numerous doctors, hospitals, therapists, and prayers, a miracle occurred. Nathan finally said, "Mommy." Jenny shared, "After six long years of waiting, Nathan is calling for me — not screaming, not yanking on my clothes. He is legitimately calling me! It started as a whisper during a late-night snuggle, but now he says my name with gusto. Sometimes it's "mommy," and other times, it's "bommy." Whatever it is — it is meant just for me. I am his mother, and he can now say my name!"

As the months continued to pass, Mark and Jenny celebrated every new word and small milestone that Nathan conquered. It was a slow process, as they lovingly watched him emerge from years of silence. His little face radiated with joy when he used the right words to express his thoughts, one word at a time.

Gradually, he was able to use his little voice to say short phrases, even though his words were hard to understand. Before long, he started to repeat parts of the Lord's Prayer with his parents. Yes, it was mumbled, and out of order, but he knew the words. Then one day, Nathan said, "Love you, too," as he hugged his Mom. Jenny's heart overflowed.

By the time Nathan turned seven, Jenny and Mark were working with several different doctors, therapists, and teachers to help their son maneuver through his developmental challenges. Nathan was still in pull-ups, struggling to speak clearly, could not read or write, and did not have "real" friends, except his family. They were also dealing with various behavior problems that stemmed from his years of "being locked-up in silence." To further complicate Nathan's situation, he was diagnosed with numerous allergies.

The constant emotional and financial strains were unbelievable. As they desperately tried to help their son, their insurance company failed to cover many of Nathan's CAS-related medical expenses. As the bills piled up, so did their anxiety. Before long, they were forced to sell their family home. So, stepping out in faith, they placed their home on the market, trusted God, and moved into a rental house. Once again, their home was filled with love.

Jenny shared, "Through every high and low, we did our best to praise God. It was a sad day when we sold our home, but we knew God was with us. As we continued to keep our hearts open to our Heavenly Father, He would reveal our next steps and open new doors. He would always help us see the 'silver lining' in the middle of our latest storm. We never felt alone, even when Nathan's seizures returned shortly after our move."

She continued, "Time and time again, God surrounded us with the right people at the right time to help us. It was amazing to watch.

Our needs, both big and small, were fulfilled by people in all areas of our lives, including family, managers, co-workers, neighbors, specialists, and priests. Even today, God continues to sustain us and provide what we need when we need it."

> *"Wait for the Lord; be strong and take heart*
> *and wait for the Lord." Psalm 27:14 (NIV)*

By the time Nathan turned ten, he had additional breakthroughs, thanks to some amazing public school teachers and specialists who recognized his capabilities and refused to "give up" on him. After many steps and observations, his school ordered an applied behavior analysis to provide additional insights on different methods to help Nathan succeed. In addition, his speech therapist performed an extensive evaluation of his progress with CAS and other challenges. As a result of the tests and analysis, Nathan's CAS diagnosis was re-confirmed. He was also classified to be on the autism spectrum and determined to have impulse control issues.

> *"Be joyful in hope, patient in affliction,*
> *faithful in prayer." Romans 12:12 (NIV)*

Thankfully, there is good news. Despite Nathan's diagnosis, God has been faithful. He is now ten years old and is "all in" for life. Jenny shared, "Even though Nathan is still hard to understand, he initiates conversations, asks questions, tells us how he feels, and what he wants to do. It is a joy to hear him sing, play the drums, and watch him run around the yard. Every month, his speech improves, and we are learning so many new things about our child. Nathan is funny, smart, lovable, patient, and loyal. He is a blessing, and I am honored to call him my son!"

Developmentally, Nathan still has a long way to go. Mark and Jenny's anxiety escalates when they think about his future. Jenny shared, "The pain of the unknown is unbearable. I go there often, but only for a moment, before fear and sadness overcome me."

"We finally saved enough money to buy a new house, but we made sure it had a basement, because what if Nathan can never live alone? What if he never graduates, gets a job, finds someone to marry? Statistically, we know the odds are against him. But we also know that with God, all things are possible."

"Therefore, do not worry about tomorrow,
for tomorrow will worry about itself.
Each day has enough trouble of its own." Matthew 6:34 (NIV)

"Having a special needs child changed our lifetime goals, how we live, and how we see the world. But through our journey with God, we found joy, compassion, empathy, new friends, and the strength to persevere. We strive to be kind to the people who cross our paths, even when we are having a tough day. Everyone is going through challenges in their lives. We need to be mindful and compassionate with one other, especially with those who have special needs."

"But the fruit of the Spirit is love, joy, peace,
patience, kindness, goodness, faithfulness,
gentleness and self-control." Galatians 5:22-23 (NIV)

In closing, Jenny shared, "God continues to be with Nathan and our entire family as we move forward and grow together. CAS didn't just happen to Nathan. It impacted our family and friends, and we are better people for being on this unplanned journey. Nathan is our hero, and we love him unconditionally. We praise God for the miracles and grace He will provide in the days to come. Amen."

"...but those who hope in the Lord will renew their strength.
They will soar on wings like eagles;
they will run and not grow weary,
they will walk and not be faint."
Isaiah 40:31 (NIV)

Author's Note: To celebrate Nathan's progress, a group of people called "Nathan's Dream Team" come together every fall to participate in the "Walk for Apraxia." His team consists of family, friends, and even teachers (both past and present) who continue to surround him with love, hope, and encouragement. Donations from the walk provide funding for apraxia research, workshops, and resources to assist parents with speech devices like iPads. Additional information about Apraxia Kids is available at www.apraxia-kids.org.

REFLECTION

Life does not always transpire the way we hoped or planned. Sometimes things do not make sense, and we get confused.

1. Pause and Reflect. Are there things in your life that did not go as planned? What happened?

_____

_____

_____

_____

_____

_____

_____

2. Did you reach out to God for strength, comfort, and guidance? What happened?

_____

_____

_____

_____

_____

_____

_____

_____

NEXT STEPS

Prayer is a powerful gift from God. Regardless of the things going on in your life, our Heavenly Father is waiting to listen to you.

Do you want to start a conversation with God right now? Skip the fancy words...just talk to Him. Openly share your thoughts, hurts, fears, failures, and hopes. Don't hesitate or be afraid. God loves YOU — unconditionally!

> *"Listen to my words, Lord, consider my lament.*
> *Hear my cry for help, my King and my God, for to you I pray...*
> *I lay my requests before you and wait expectantly."*
> *Psalm 5:1-3 (NIV)*

CLOSING PRAYER

Dear Heavenly Father,

Life is not always easy, and there are so many things that I don't understand. Please help me navigate through the challenges in my life. When I'm overwhelmed and unsure of what to do, please gently guide me in the right direction. Help me to embrace your strength, peace, and wisdom, as I press forward to accomplish your purpose for my life. I love you. Amen.

The Blessings of a God-Centered Marriage

"Love always protects, always trusts,
always hopes, always perseveres."
1 Corinthians 13:7 (NIV)

The doctor entered the room, holding Mary's biopsy results. After a short pause, he shared the dreaded news, "You have cancer. There are two spots on your right breast; both require surgery. I recommend the full removal of your right breast." Mary took a deep breath, then quietly glanced at her husband. The cancer diagnosis was the latest challenge they would bravely face together.

Mary and Dan first met in the fall of 1988 while attending the same church. Mary was new to the area and enjoyed an instant connection with Dan. Within a few weeks, they started to date. From the beginning, God was in the center of their relationship. They worshiped together every Sunday and served in various leadership roles at their church. They regularly prayed for each other and their relationship. After a whirlwind romance, including an engagement four months after they met, Mary and Dan married in August of 1989.

"Therefore, what God has joined together, let no one separate."
Mark 10:9 (NIV)

The first eighteen months of their marriage were relatively carefree. They were excited about their careers, their future, and each other. Then, unplanned heartbreaks and storms began to enter their lives.

In the spring of 1991, Mary began to experience flashbacks regarding abuse she endured as a child, things she previously blocked from her memory. As her gut-wrenching memories unfolded, Dan prayed for Mary and encouraged her to seek professional help to deal with her "new reality." As a result, she was hospitalized for two weeks and received the focused counseling and support she desperately needed.

> *"Husbands, love your wives, just as Christ*
> *loved the church and gave himself up for her."*
> *Ephesians 5:25 (NIV)*

When Mary left the hospital, Dan continued to support her with love and compassion. Together, they held on to God's promises, because they knew He had a purpose for their lives and marriage. As the months passed, God began to heal Mary's emotional scars and the violations she endured as a child.

> *"I have come into the world as a light,*
> *so that no one who believes in me should*
> *stay in darkness." John 12:46 (NIV)*

As life moved on, Mary and Dan received exciting news — they would soon be parents! Unfortunately, their happy news shattered when Mary had a miscarriage followed by another, and then another. But through their heartbreaks and sadness, they continued to support and console each other as they leaned on God for strength and peace.

> *"Peace I leave with you; my peace I give you.*
> *I do not give to you as the world gives.*
> *Do not let your hearts be troubled and do not be afraid."*
> *John 14:27 (NIV)*

In May of 1993, Mary was pregnant once again. They were cautiously optimistic but realized there could be another miscarriage. Fortunately, as the months passed, her pregnancy was viable, and their baby began to grow. Just as they started to breathe a sigh of relief, some concerns surfaced at the beginning of her sixth month, so her doctor ordered an amniocentesis. The test results indicated their baby had a chromosome abnormality.

Dan and Mary were devastated, confused, and heartbroken. They wondered why this happened, but they also knew God was with them and loved their baby. They continued to pray for their unborn child, and the emotional strength to deal with this unplanned situation. Together, they prepared for the unknown and a tough journey, as their family, friends, and church encircled them in prayer.

Given the diagnosis, the doctors reviewed the various next steps and options available. Dan and Mary chose to continue the pregnancy, realizing there was a significant developmental problem with their baby. Early termination of her pregnancy was not an option they were willing to consider.

"For I know the plans I have for you," declares the Lord,
"plans to prosper you and not to harm you,
plans to give you hope and a future." Jeremiah 29:11 (NIV)

Over the next several weeks, they did their best to remain hopeful. Then, some unexpected information jolted their world. Through DNA testing, they learned Mary passed a rare abnormal gene to their unborn baby daughter. Overwhelmed with guilt, she proactively began counseling sessions with her pastor to work through her feelings. She realized the guilt was not from God, but just another way the adversary was trying to attack and break her.

"So do not fear, for I am with you; do not be dismayed,
for I am your God. I will strengthen you and help you;
I will uphold you with my righteous right hand."
Isaiah 41:10 (NIV)

As Mary's pregnancy continued, Dan did everything possible to support her while dealing with debilitating stress migraines. Despite their situation, they continued to comfort each other by listening with compassion, taking long walks, holding hands, and praying. Mary shared, "God had us in the palm of His hand. He gave us the strength to move forward, the right words to comfort each other, and the ability to deal with the mental exhaustion. We replaced our fear with faith in our Heavenly Father."

On February 2, 1994, the doctors performed a c-section and delivered their beautiful baby girl named Grace. Mary and Dan briefly held and kissed their daughter before she was airlifted 150 miles away to a top children's hospital, which specialized in newborns with chromosome abnormalities. Grace was losing blood, had dislocated hips, and there was a hole between the ventricles in her heart.

Little Grace faced an uphill battle. Numerous machines kept her alive as the doctors frantically worked to stabilize her condition. They performed a life-saving heart surgery when she was only two weeks old, but the doctors knew she faced numerous challenges. It was at that time, Dan reluctantly asked the tough question, "How long do we keep this going?" Mary lovingly replied, "Until God tells us otherwise."

> *"The Lord is close to the brokenhearted*
> *and saves those who are crushed in spirit."*
> *Psalm 34:18 (NIV)*

Finally, after four weeks, the doctors stabilized Grace just long enough to conduct an MRI scan. Regardless of the outcome, they knew their unborn baby was a child of God, and He would love and care for her, either here on earth or in heaven. Unfortunately, the scan results were devastating. Grace's brain did not fully develop. The automatic functions to control her body, including her breathing, were missing.

> *"Blessed are those who mourn, for they will be comforted."*
> *Matthew 5:4 (NIV)*

The doctors soon delivered heartbreaking news, "We are so sorry. There is nothing else we can do for your baby." At that moment, Mary knew it was the sign from God to let her go. At twenty-nine days old, baby Grace quietly passed away into the loving arms of Jesus.

Jesus said, "Let the little children come to me,
and do not hinder them, for the kingdom of
heaven belongs to such as these."
Matthew 19:14 (NIV)

God surrounded Mary and Dan with friends and family as they mourned the death of their baby. Mary shared, "During our journey with Grace, God provided the right people, at the right time, to provide exactly what we needed. It was amazing to watch Him fulfill our needs through others. God carried us during the darkest time of our lives."

The weeks following Grace's death were indescribably sad. Thankfully, they had each other, and God's ever-present peace to sustain them. Mary shared, "I am so thankful God was with us through this heartbreaking time. Without Him, I do not know how I would have survived the gut-wrenching, emotional pain I experienced. Our Heavenly Father understood my heartbreak and comforted me, just like a Father comforts their child. Despite my sorrow, God filled my heart with an indescribable peace. I will forever be grateful."

"And the peace of God, which transcends all understanding,
will guard your hearts and your minds in Christ Jesus."
Philippians 4:7 (NIV)

She went on to share, "We don't know why Grace's life unfolded the way it did, but we do know that God is good, just, loving, and compassionate. We live in a fallen world full of pain, sorrow, disease, and death. Everyone will eventually pass away from this life, but God called Grace home much earlier than we ever expected. However, there is good news and hope. Thanks to the grace of God and the gift of eternal life, I know we will see Grace again."

"For God so loved the world,
that he gave his only begotten Son,
that whosoever believeth in him should not perish,
but have everlasting life." John 3:16 (KJV)

As the months passed, Dan and Mary began to turn their focus toward the future, and the possibility of another child. After many appointments and tests, their doctors and DNA specialists reassured them — it was safe to get pregnant again. The probability of the rare gene passing to another child was extremely remote. With that assurance, they once again replaced their fear with faith and moved forward.

> *"May the God of hope fill you with all joy and peace*
> *as you trust in him, so that you may overflow with hope*
> *by the power of the Holy Spirit." Romans 15:13 (NIV)*

Mary became pregnant in the fall of 1994. Throughout her pregnancy, they trusted God and embraced His love and peace. In June 1995, she delivered a healthy baby boy named Mark — there were no complications. Together, they praised God as their hearts overflowed with love and gratitude.

> *"And now these three remain: faith, hope, and love.*
> *But the greatest of these is love."*
> *1 Corinthians 13:13 (NIV)*

The following five years were a time of restoration. Yes, there were some ups and downs, but for the most part, life was relatively calm. Then in 1999, Mary delivered another healthy, little boy named Luke. They were thrilled.

As the hours passed in the hospital, Mary noticed their baby was very unsettled, and she sensed their journey with little Luke might hold some challenges. So, as she had done many times before, Mary prayed. She knew God had a purpose for Luke's life, as her heart filled with hope.

> *"Now faith is confidence in what we hope for*
> *and assurance about what we do not see."*
> *Hebrews 11:1 (NIV)*

As the years continued to pass, Mark excelled in school, and things came easily to him, while his little brother Luke struggled. Dan and Mary never panicked as they faced reality, trusted God, and sought professional help for their son. God once again blanketed them with His indescribable peace as they discovered Luke had:

- A growth hormone deficiency which impacted his ability to grow
- A short-term auditory learning disability
- Attention Deficit Hyperactivity Disorder (ADHD)
- Anxiety disorders

Dan and Mary encircled Luke with love, as doctors and specialists diagnosed each new challenge. They continued to lean on each other and asked God for strength and direction. In 2008, Luke began treatments to counteract his growth hormone deficiency. The successful treatments continued for ten years. He also received special services from the school district for his other challenges.

In 2011, Mary and Dan decided to raise and train "Guide Dogs for the Blind" as a method to offer service to others, while helping Luke with some of his challenges. The guide dog program was a huge blessing for the entire family, and the dogs had a calming effect on Luke. The program also provided the opportunity to connect with new groups of people.

*"You, Lord, keep my lamp burning; my God
turns my darkness into light." Psalm 18:28 (NIV)*

In 2013, Mark graduated from high school and headed to college, while Luke entered his freshman year in high school. Then, for some unknown reason, storms started to bombard Mary and Dan's family once again. Mary shared, "Just because you are a Christian and believe in God does not mean you are exempt from bad things happening in your life. We know we will have trouble here on earth, but as we have learned firsthand, God will carry us through our storms."

*"I have told you these things,
so that in me you may have peace.
In this world you will have trouble. But take heart!
I have overcome the world." John 16:33 (NIV)*

In the spring of 2014, Luke was diagnosed with Autism Spectrum Disorder (ASD) and began receiving additional specialized support. Then, in the summer of 2014, Mary's mother fell. Despite numerous attempts to rehabilitate her, she passed away during the winter of 2015. Once again, Mary was heartbroken.

Then, in the summer of 2015, just as Mary began to "get her feet on the ground," she went in for her annual mammogram. A few days later, she received a call stating they needed additional images, which were followed by an ultrasound, biopsy, and MRI scan. Mary was alarmed since her mother previously had Stage 3 breast cancer, but she also knew God and her husband would support her, no matter what the diagnosis revealed.

After the tests were complete, Dan and Mary had an appointment with the oncologist. When the doctor entered the room, holding the biopsy results, he shared the dreaded news, "You have cancer. There are two spots on your right breast; both require surgery. I recommend the full removal of your right breast." Mary took a deep breath, then quietly looked at her husband. She knew God would carry them through this storm.

*"Trust in the Lord with all your heart
and lean not on your own understanding..."*
Proverbs 3:5 (NIV)

Due to her family history, Mary and Dan jointly decided on a double mastectomy. Mary was concerned about losing part of her body and femininity, but in her head, she heard God say, "I've got this." From that point forward, Mary had complete peace regarding her situation. Thanks to the early detection of her cancer — radiation and chemotherapy were not required.

"Be joyful in hope, patient in affliction, faithful in prayer."
Romans 12:12 (NIV)

In the summer of 2016, Mary's father passed away, followed by the death of another family member a few months later. Sadness once again filled Mary's heart, but she never lost hope. Like prior times in their lives, Dan and Mary climbed out of the valley of storms and were once again able to rest. Mary shared, "No matter what trials or heartbreaks we face, God is an ever-present light as he guides our paths to heaven. We just need to believe and trust Him."

"The light shines in the darkness, and the darkness
has not overcome it." John 1:5 (NIV)

Mark went on to graduate from college and is working full time. He is a compassionate person and a devoted son. Luke graduated from high school, attends the local community college, has a landscaping job, and drives a car. Given the challenges he faced during his childhood, Luke is a miracle. Anyone who has the opportunity to meet these young men notice the radiant love they share with others. God's love shines through them.

"Do everything in love." 1 Corinthians 16:14 (NIV)

In closing, Mary shared, "Dan and my boys are a blessing from God, and I am grateful. We recently celebrated the thirtieth anniversary of our God-centered marriage. When we pause and reflect on our tough times, we are amazed at the various ways God surrounded us with just the right people at the right time to sustain us. If you are going through tough times in your life, remember to look up! God is calling your name and is ready to help you. Praise God!"

A special two-sided coin that Mary carries in her purse.

REFLECTION

As we saw in Mary and Dan's journey, their God-centered marriage includes several key attributes:

- They have an individual and personal relationship with God.
- They trust God.
- Through prayer, they seek God's direction and guidance for their lives.
- They respect, support, and pray for each other during the good and tough times.

Pause and Reflect.

1. Are you currently married? If yes, how does your marriage reflect the attributes listed above?

_____

_____

_____

2. If you are not married, what can you learn from Dan and Mary's God-centered marriage?

_____

_____

_____

3. Can you identify some things that would deepen your relationship with God?

_____

_____

_____

NEXT STEPS

Heartbreaks, death, illnesses, and tough times are part of life. Thankfully, you do not need to face life's challenges alone. God will carry you through the rough times.

Pause for a moment. List some specific things in your life where you want or need God's help today.

_____

_____

_____

_____

_____

_____

_____

_____

CLOSING PRAYER

Dear Heavenly Father,

Thank you for loving me. I need your help and comfort today. Can you please help me with _____? I can no longer do this by myself. Thank you for giving me hope. Amen.

Living Through a 7.1 Earthquake

"...And surely I am with you always, to the very end of the age."
Matthew 28:20 (NIV)

Without notice, the floor began to shake. Seconds later, items in the local store began to tumble off the shelves. As the shaking intensified, glass bottles shattered, and plastic containers burst open as they plunged to the floor. Barbara quickly realized — this was not a "routine" California earthquake. What was she going to do?

Thursday, July 4th

It was a typical fourth of July in Ridgecrest, California; the sun was shining, with a warm forecast of ninety-eight degrees. Located in the Mojave Desert, Ridgecrest is in the Indian Wells Valley, at the base of the Sierra Nevada Mountains. Approximately 28,000 people call this unique town their home.

Barbara, a long-time Ridgecrest resident, decided to get up early to run a few errands before enjoying hot dogs and ice cream, as part of her usual July 4th celebration. A little after 10:15 AM, she entered the local Dollar Tree store, as she had done many times before. She had no idea of the events that would unfold over the following minutes.

Barbara passed some other customers as she weaved back and forth through the aisles, making her way to the greeting card section. After finding just the right cards for some upcoming birthdays, she pushed her cart toward the back of the store to pick up some cleaning supplies.

Suddenly, Barbara heard a loud rumbling sound, and the floor started to shake. As the trembling intensified, the ground felt as if it was rolling, and items began to tumble off the shelves. The scene inside the store became confusing and chaotic. Then, for some reason, Barbara glanced up and noticed the wall unit that held the household cleaning supplies was rocking and separating from the wall.

As the shaking continued to strengthen, the wall unit began to lean forward, then started to fall, right where Barbara was standing. She shared, "I saw it falling and knew I had to get out of the way." In a split second, she took a few quick steps toward a center aisle, just before the unit crashed to the floor, and the lights went out. The sound of bottles breaking was deafening as cleaning fluid from the broken bottles splashed all over her pant legs. The store was completely dark as the shaking and shattering of bottles finally subsided.

> *"...In this world you will have trouble. But take heart!*
> *I have overcome the world." John 16:33 (NIV)*

Barbara was dizzy and felt unsteady from the violent earthquake, but knew she had to get out of the store. It was pitch black, and debris was everywhere. For a brief moment, she was paralyzed in fear, unsure of what to do next. Then, in the chaos, as she held tightly to her shopping cart, Barbara heard two voices frantically yelling, "Where is she? Where is she? — I don't know. I can't find her." Without hesitation, Barbara yelled, "I'm here. I'm here." She immediately knew that despite the earthquake, God sent people to help her.

> *"God is our refuge and strength, an ever-present*
> *help in trouble. Therefore, we will not fear,*
> *though the earth give way..." Psalm 46:1-2 (NIV)*

A few seconds later, a man and woman, who were shopping in the back of the store, found Barbara in the dark, by following her voice. The strangers asked if she was okay, then developed a quick "game plan" to get out of the store. The man gently guided her cart, one step at a time, while the woman walked a few feet ahead, feeling her way down the aisle and pushing debris away with her feet, attempting to make a small pathway. As they came closer to the front of the store, they could see sunlight shining through an unbroken window. Glass was everywhere. Barbara gratefully thanked the man and woman for their help, then carefully walked out of the store with her cane.

> *"The light shines in the darkness,*
> *and the darkness has not overcome it."*
> *John 1:5 (NIV)*

The ground was still moving when the warm sun hit Barbara's face. As her eyes adjusted to the daylight, she saw several people gathered outside the store — they were in a state of shock, and their faces were full of fear. Barbara knew she needed to get home, so she stabilized herself with her cane and walked to her car. The earth was still moving.

As she sat quietly in her car and tried to gather her thoughts, the car began to jerk back and forth from another earthquake. She was physically shaking as she started the car and drove home in a daze. When Barbara arrived at her house, she was met by several neighbors who were gathered outside, consoling each other. It was at this point she learned a 6.4 magnitude earthquake hit the town, the largest earthquake to strike California in twenty years. Sirens were screaming in the distance, and smoke began to fill the clear blue sky.

Despite the damage in their own homes, several neighbors joined their ninety-year-old friend, Barbara, as she slowly opened her front door and stepped inside. The house had no electricity and was very warm since the air conditioner was off. At first glance, she saw lamps thrown on the carpet and tipped over pictures. As she stepped further into her home, Barbara gasped when she saw the devastation in her kitchen and family room. The kitchen cabinets flew open during the massive earthquake. Shattered dishes now blanketed the countertops and floor.

The family room was a disaster. The powerful earthquake knocked over bookcases, file cabinets, and antique furniture. There were piles of broken family heirlooms, some pieces dating back to the 1800s. For a split second, Barbara's heart broke as she gazed at the broken teacups and beautiful dishes that belonged to her mother, but she snapped back to reality as the earth began to move once again. She then said to her neighbors, "They were just things. Thankfully, no one was injured." From that point forward, she let go of her losses, focused on God, and the people around her.

"For where your treasure is,
there your heart will be also." Luke 12:34 (NIV)

For the next hour, her neighbors gently sifted through her piles of rubble, celebrating when they found a teacup or dish that survived the quake. Before long, they filled two large dumpsters with broken glass. Some pieces of furniture were crushed and unable to be salvaged. The bedrooms also contained several damaged items, but again, they were just material things.

Barbara was overwhelmed and grateful for the outpouring of love and support she received. She was astounded that neighbors focused on her needs first, before turning their attention toward their damaged homes. Love and compassion overflowed in her neighborhood.

"...Love your neighbor as yourself..."
Mark 12:31 (NIV)

That afternoon, the ground continued to shake from aftershocks, as friends from her church and extended family stopped by to ensure she was okay. Barbara's daughters, who were on the east coast, reached her by cell phone as they continued to pray for her safety, as well as the people in the entire town of Ridgecrest and outlying areas. Seismologists warned that large aftershocks would occur, and there was a possibility a more powerful earthquake could hit the area.

When evening drew near, Barbara enjoyed an unplanned 4th of July dinner at the home of her extended family. As they prayed at the dinner table for their evening meal, they thanked God for keeping them safe. Throughout dinner, they did their best to maintain upbeat conversations, as the earth continued to move beneath their feet. They invited Barbara to spend the night, but she decided to be tough and sleep in her own home since the power company restored her electricity.

That night, Barbara stayed in her clothes and slept in the reclining chair near her front door, in case another massive earthquake struck. She once again thanked God for protecting her and placed her fate in His hands. Unfortunately, sleep eluded her most of the night, as her human heart and mind rushed each time another aftershock rumbled through her house.

Friday, July 5th

Early the next morning, a 5.4 aftershock hit the entire area. It set the tone for the rest of the day. People were nervous as the earth continued to shake. Barbara shared, "As I felt each quake under my feet, I wondered if it would get stronger and how long it would last. I found myself feeling dizzy most of the day due to the persistent movement. It was unsettling."

> *"Do not be anxious about anything, but in every situation, by prayer and petition, with thanksgiving, present your requests to God." Philippians 4:6 (NIV)*

Despite the aftershocks, Barbara and the rest of the town continued clean-up efforts as they tried to move forward with their day. Most businesses remained closed due to damage, so people gathered where they could and shared their stories. People across the small community were kind, helpful, and concerned for each other. It was as if the earthquake "brought out the best" in everyone.

That evening, Barbara decided to sleep in her clothes once again as she nestled into her reclining chair. She carefully placed a flashlight and her purse close by, just in case she needed them. Exhausted from watching the news coverage of the earthquake, Barbara turned the channel to Jeopardy, then flipped to the Hallmark Channel in an attempt to keep things positive. As she glanced out her front window, the sun was setting in the west, and all was quiet.

Suddenly, at 8:16 PM, a 5.0 quake rattled her entire house. It alarmed her. Then, at 8:19 PM, she heard a horrific noise, and loud rumbling as the floor began to shake violently. Confused, she struggled to get out of her chair and walk to the kitchen. Then, all the lights in the house went out.

The shaking and jerking continued to intensify as she held on to her kitchen table. It was hard to comprehend what was happening. The earth's violent and frightening movements were unlike any-thing she ever experienced. The walls, ceilings, and floor in the house moved as if they were alive. It was almost like an out of body experience as items flew across the room, crashed on the floor, and swayed back and forth.

As glassware shattered, Barbara continued to hold on to the table for dear life and cried out, "God, I can't stay here. I can't stay here." Finally, after what felt like an eternity, the jerking and shaking began to subside. Afraid to move, she slowly looked around her house in a state of shock as the ground was still moving. White particles of dust filled the air; it resembled fog.

> *"The Lord is my rock, my fortress and my deliverer;*
> *my God is my rock, in whom I take refuge..."*
> *Psalm 18:2 (NIV)*

A few seconds later, Barbara heard someone pounding on her front door and yelling, "You have to get out. You have to get out." Somehow, Barbara managed to get to the front door and open it. Her neighbor quickly grabbed her arm and said, "You have to get out." Barbara grabbed her purse, hugged her neighbor, and walked out.

The trauma of the 7.1 magnitude earthquake did not stop there. For the next hour, the earth continued to move as hundreds of quakes struck the area. Some of the higher magnitude aftershocks, as seen below, continued to shatter nerves, as sirens filled the evening air.

7.1 Ridgecrest Earthquake and the First Hour of Large Aftershocks

8:19 PM – 7.1 Earthquake	8:28 PM – 4.3 Aftershock	8:47 PM – 5.5 Aftershock
8.22 PM – 4.6 Aftershock	8:29 PM – 4.5 Aftershock	8:50 PM – 4.9 Aftershock
8:22 PM – 5.0 Aftershock	8:30 PM – 4.5 Aftershock	8:55 PM – 4.1 Aftershock
8:23 PM – 5.4 Aftershock	8:32 PM – 4.2 Aftershock	8:57 PM – 4.3 Aftershock
8:24 PM – 4.3 Aftershock	8:36 PM – 4.2 Aftershock	9:07 PM – 5.0 Aftershock
8:25 PM – 5.0 Aftershock	8:41 PM – 4.0 Aftershock	9:13 PM – 4.8 Aftershock
8:27 PM – 4.7 Aftershock	8:44 PM – 4.0 Aftershock	9:18 PM – 5.4 Aftershock
8:28 PM – 4.1 Aftershock	8:46 PM – 4.2 Aftershock	9:19 PM – 4.2 Aftershock

People were in their front yards, afraid to go back into their homes. Before long, members of Barbara's family came to assess her situation and take her to their home, just a few miles away. Before leaving, they entered Barbara's house and maneuvered through the glass and debris so she could quickly pack a small overnight bag. When they closed her front door, they could hear glass breaking as the earth continued to shake.

Despite the earthquakes, it was a beautiful desert night. The stars glistened in the clear sky, and the night temperature was comfortable. For safety reasons, Barbara and five members of her family decided to "camp out" in the front yard, away from falling objects.

Barbara shared, "I was so grateful to be with members of my family versus staying in my dark house all alone. We slept on the front lawn in chairs and had a blow-up mattress. Some neighbors pitched tents as police and firefighters diligently patrolled the neighborhood throughout the night. We could hear helicopters flying overhead as they attempted to assess the damage."

She continued, "As the shaking carried on, we did our best to comfort each other, and on occasion, found ourselves breaking out in laughter as we enjoyed each other's company. What could have been a terrifying night was surprisingly pleasant and enjoyable. We managed to get a few hours of sleep, in-between the rocking and rolling of the earth below us."

> *"Peace I leave with you; my peace I give you.*
> *I do not give to you as the world gives. Do not let*
> *your hearts be troubled and do not be afraid."*
> *John 14:27 (NIV)*

Saturday, July 6th

As the sun began to rise on Saturday morning, people were grateful they survived the night. Daylight revealed widespread damage to businesses and homes throughout the area. Many employers remained closed as they removed debris and checked for structural issues. Some residents lost their homes due to fires, but thankfully, no one in the local community died as a result of the earthquakes. Residents were shocked to learn the massive earthquakes left large, visible cracks in the earth's surface — fractures that were visible from space.

As the clean-up process started once again, caring people from various parts of the country, including the national guard, police, and firefighters, came to assist. Kindness and love overflowed throughout the small community. Strangers reached out to strangers, neighbors helped neighbors, and families grew closer together.

> *"And now these three remain: faith, hope, and love.*
> *But the greatest of these is love." 1 Corinthians 13:13 (NIV)*

Sunday, July 7th

On Sunday morning, Barbara attended her local church. She watched as people greeted each other with hugs and exchanged their stories from the past seventy-two hours. As the morning church service began, the pastor reviewed the safety procedures in the event a sizeable earthquake struck once again. Then the church family sang songs of praise and offered prayers of thanksgiving to their Heavenly Father.

Tuesday, July 9th

The strong aftershocks finally began to subside. Barbara returned to her home. The structure of her house survived, but the "emotional safety net" was different. For the next several nights, she continued to sleep near the front door in her clothes. She knew God was with her, but also felt she needed to be vigilant.

In reflecting over the ten-thousand earthquakes that hit Ridgecrest in the span of one week, Barbara said, "It isn't the things we lost that people should focus on. It's the blessings of how people came together to help each other, whether it be picking up broken glass, fixing air conditioners, sharing a meal, providing water, or offering a hug of encouragement. I will forever be grateful to my wonderful neighbors and extended family who came to my aid during my time of need. Their service above self was abundantly clear and appreciated."

"Carry each other's burdens, and in this way
you will fulfill the law of Christ." Galatians 6:2 (NIV)

In closing, she shared, "I don't know when I will take my last breath or when the next big earthquake will strike. However, I am certain of this. God is with us all the time, and I am grateful. If you are going through uncertain times, pause, and ask God to help you. He will carry you through the shaky times of your life, just like He carried me."

"Therefore, do not worry about tomorrow,
for tomorrow will worry about itself.
Each day has enough trouble of its own."
Matthew 6:34 (NIV)

Sleeping outside – Morning after the 7.1 Earthquake

Barbara's heirloom dishes from her Mother

REFLECTION

Living through a natural disaster can be very frightening. Since we live in a fallen world, natural disasters occur every day, including earthquakes, volcanic eruptions, hurricanes, cyclones, tornadoes, blizzards, avalanches, tsunamis, floods, mudslides, and wildfires.

1. Have you lived through a natural disaster, or do you know someone who survived a natural disaster? What happened?

_____

_____

_____

_____

_____

_____

2. How did God help during and after the disaster?

_____

_____

_____

_____

_____

_____

NEXT STEPS

Natural disasters, accidents, or sudden illnesses can shake our confidence and force us to reflect on our lives. Sometimes we have advanced notice, such as an impending storm, but sometimes we find ourselves facing unexpected situations. For example, an earthquake or a heart attack can strike without warning. Take a few minutes and reflect:

1. If you died tomorrow due to a natural disaster, accident, or illness, are you confident your life is right with God? If not, are there some proactive steps you want to take to "get your life in order?"

    _____

    _____

    _____

    _____

2. Are there some specific things you need to stop doing? List those items below:

    _____

    _____

    _____

    _____

3. Are there some things you want to start doing? List those items below:

    _____

    _____

    _____

    _____

CLOSING PRAYER

Dear Heavenly Father,

Natural disasters, accidents, and sudden illnesses happen every day. I realize there is no guarantee I will live to see tomorrow. Please examine my life and heart. Show me the things I need to change to ensure I am living my life according to your purpose for me here on earth. Amen.

Raising My Grandchild

Jesus said, "Let the little children come to me,
and do not hinder them, for the kingdom
of heaven belongs to such as these."
Matthew 19:14 (NIV)

The doorbell rang. Vicky's biological father was standing at the front door, holding a handful of "official-looking" papers. Cathy had not seen him for ten years. As her pulse began to race and heart started to break, he shared his gut-wrenching news that changed their lives forever.

It was a beautiful summer weekend in Seattle. Cathy and her husband were happily married and enjoying life with their two teenage daughters. Their daughters were grateful for the summer break from school. Life was calm, with no real challenges or issues.

As the summer progressed, their youngest daughter Debbie received an invitation to sleep-over at her friend's house. Cathy agreed since she knew Debbie's friend and her parents. There were no "red flags" or any reasons for concern. Regrettably, Cathy's trust was misplaced.

The night of the sleep-over, Debbie found herself in a car with her friend's drunk mother. As this woman drove erratically, with no regard for the girls in the car, she hit a tree. Fortunately, no one appeared to be injured, but the vehicle sustained substantial damage. At some point, they left the car at the site of the accident, and someone drove them back to her friend's house. Alarmingly, no one called the police or Cathy.

The next morning, Cathy received a call from the mother, who was now sober. She said, "We had a little accident." Cathy immediately picked up her daughter, who shared the details about the incident. As they were driving home, Debbie complained about a pain in her back, and the left side of her body was numb, so Cathy took her to the emergency room. The doctors discovered, in addition to her pain and numbness, she sustained a concussion. Unfortunately, her pain continued to intensify, so the doctors prescribed an opioid to ease her discomfort. Cathy shared, "This prescription was the start of addiction entering our lives. It just snuck in and caught all of us by surprise."

"The thief comes only to steal and kill and destroy..."
John 10:10 (NIV)

Over the next few months, Debbie's behavior started to change. At first, she claimed to be sick and missed several days from school. Cathy attributed this to the accident. However, as time passed, their sweet daughter started to transform right before their eyes. She became argumentative with extreme "up and down" mood swings, and before long, began to ditch school. Her parents were unaware that her prescription drug use escalated to buying opioid drugs from classmates. Unfortunately, her drug habit quickly spiraled out of control and expanded to other illegal drugs.

"Be alert and of sober mind. Your enemy, the devil,
prowls around like a roaring lion looking for someone to devour."
1 Peter 5:8 (NIV)

By age sixteen, Debbie's parent's found illegal drugs in her bedroom. They were horrified as they watched their once innocent, beautiful daughter now trapped in a vicious drug addiction, which included methamphetamines. Cathy and her husband did not know what to do, or where to turn. Before long, their daughter was facing time in juvenile hall, but Debbie did not care. Her goal in life was to "get high" and find her next "fix."

Debbie dropped out of high school and began attending an alternative school for problem teens. Despite all odds, she graduated as her drug use intensified. Unfortunately, illegal drugs now controlled her moral compass and caused additional stress in her family. Her sister had "broken-up" with her longtime, atheist boyfriend named Mark. Debbie thought it would be fun to hang out with him but took it a step further. She slept with Mark and became pregnant.

Debbie's sister was outraged, hurt, and angry. Cathy felt trapped between her two daughters, and the situation was overwhelming. Powerless, she strived to keep peace in her family. Debbie tried to explain, "it was just an accident because I already have a boyfriend." The drugs distorted her values.

Cathy and her husband did their best to console and empathize with their oldest daughter, while also focusing on eighteen-year-old Debbie and her unborn child. Debbie continued living with her boyfriend, but their relationship was in turmoil due to her pregnancy and their drug addictions. She tried to stop using drugs until her baby was born, but there were times she "gave in" to her addiction.

At age nineteen, Debbie delivered a little girl named Victoria, and they called her Vicky. Vicky was healthy and showed no signs of drug-related issues. Two months later, Debbie left her boyfriend and moved back home with her parents. Mark, Vicky's biological father, desired to be part of his daughter's life, but he had limited resources and other issues. Mark disappeared from Vicky's life. During this time, Debbie's drug use intensified from methamphetamines to heroin.

Cathy and her husband lovingly cared for Vicky, as Debbie's life became more and more chaotic. She would disappear for days at a time, strung out on drugs. Her addiction was a vicious cycle. Finally, when Vicky was eight months old, Debbie's parents went to court and obtained formal guardianship.

Cathy loved being a grandmother and shared a strong bond with Vicky. She wanted her granddaughter to grow-up, knowing God, especially given Debbie's tumultuous lifestyle. Cathy regretted that her daughters did not have a relationship with God, and she did not want to repeat this mistake.

Cathy shared, "I decided to invite God into all areas of Vicky's life. She attended a Christian Day Care, Sunday School, and church. We prayed together, sang songs, and talked about our Heavenly Father. Every morning, I would go into Vicky's room, turn on the lights, and sing the old song "Rise and Shine, and give God the Glory." It was a fun tradition that started each new day with God and a smile."

"Start children off on the way they should go, and even when they are old they will not turn from it." Proverbs 22:6 (NIV)

Cathy worked diligently to keep Vicky safe in a loving and stable environment, while Debbie received help. She hoped and prayed Debbie would eventually break free from her addiction and fulfill her "mother role" to Vicky. Cathy ensured her granddaughter understood that Debbie was her mother. She would explain to little Vicky that her mommy was sick or not feeling well.

For the next two years, Debbie jumped in and out of rehab centers trying to overcome her addiction, but heroin had a powerful hold on her body, mind, and soul. Cathy shared, "It might sound terrible, but I relaxed when my daughter was in rehab because I knew she was safe." After many months of ups and downs, Debbie's life started to stabilize when she entered a Suboxone Program, which suppressed the effects of opiate drugs. Finally, she claimed to be "clean" as her life calmed down.

By this time, the courts asked Cathy and her husband to adopt Vicky, but this did not feel right. Cathy's grandmother raised her, and she remembered missing her mother. She believed Vicky should grow up with her mother if at all possible, so they relinquished their guardianship rights back to Debbie and monitored the situation carefully.

Debbie stayed off drugs as she continued to live with her parents and Vicky. She went back to school to become a medical assistant and landed a job in a medical office. Life appeared to be normalizing. Unfortunately, Debbie started complaining to one of the doctors about her back and neck pain from an old injury. The doctor prescribed pain medication, and she was immediately addicted.

Within a matter of days, Debbie disappeared on a drug binge with a man who worked in her office. For the next three weeks, no knew their whereabouts until Debbie was pulled over by the police, and they found heroin in her car. She was thrown into jail and lost her job.

Cathy and her husband went back to court and obtained guardianship for Vicky. Their decision hurt Debbie's feelings, but they needed to keep their granddaughter safe. After Debbie lost custody once again, she tried to "get clean" by going to counselors, rehab centers, 12-step programs, and also enrolled in another Suboxone Program. Withdrawals were brutal, and life was tough.

During this time, Debbie unexpectedly reached out to Mark. She thought it would be nice if he met his daughter. So, at age five, Vicky met her biological father for the first time. From that point forward, Mark would see Vicky a few times a year, but Cathy never saw him. He still had issues and was now an alcoholic.

For the next two years, Debbie was in and out of treatment programs. Blinded by the love for her daughter, Cathy continued to pay thousands of dollars for rehab centers. The entire situation placed a significant strain on their marriage. Debbie finally entered a center that specialized in opioid addictions and began to improve. She faced a long recovery journey.

By the time Vicky was eight years old, Debbie was doing well, so Cathy and her husband once again relinquished their legal guardianship rights back to their daughter. Debbie was living with her boyfriend and wanted Vicky to join them, but her daughter preferred living with her grandparents — it was her home. She was a happy girl and stayed very involved with her Christian school, gymnastics, and cheerleading.

> *"Finally, be strong in the Lord*
> *and in his mighty power." Ephesians 6:10 (NIV)*

Cathy thought Debbie was no longer under the influence of drugs, but she was wrong. One night when Debbie was with her boyfriend, she "lost her mind" while shooting heroin. She grabbed a knife and tried to stab her boyfriend before attempting to commit suicide. Her boyfriend panicked and dialed 911, but Debbie fled their apartment before the police arrived. The situation was a mess. Fortunately, Vicky was with her grandparents, tucked safely in her bed, and unaware of the nightmare she would soon face.

Mark's parents lived nearby and heard about Debbie's drug-induced meltdown. They immediately informed their son about the situation. For the next few months, they helped Mark prepare a plan to gain custody of his daughter. He took a paternity test to prove he was Vicky's biological father, then went to court, armed with Debbie's documented heroin addiction.

Cathy had no idea Mark was pursuing formal guardianship for Vicky. To make the situation worse, she did not fully understand the rights of grandparents in the state where she resided. Grandparents had no legal rights regarding their grandchildren if they did not have legal custody — custody she gave back to Debbie. The events that followed, completely blindsided Cathy, Vicky, and her family.

Cathy was home with Vicky, and the doorbell rang. As she opened the door, Mark was standing there, holding a handful of official-looking papers. She had not seen him for ten years and was alarmed. As her pulse began to race, he shared his gut-wrenching news that changed their lives forever. He was now the legal guardian for Vicky.

Cathy's mind began to race as Mark continued to talk. She thought, "This can't be. I've got to go back to court. He doesn't know my granddaughter; he has never paid child support, never given Vicky a Christmas gift, or even acknowledged her birthdays." She was overwhelmed as she tried to process the situation.

Cathy assumed Mark would slowly transition Vicky to his house, but he had a different plan. He established ground rules for future communications with Vicky, then stated he would be taking her immediately. Cathy's hands were tied due to the court order. In a matter of minutes, their world blew up, and there was nothing she could do.

Cathy was dying inside but knew she must be strong for her grand-daughter. She told Vicky, "Your Dad loves and misses you. So, he is taking you on a fun adventure to his house. You get to spend time with his other daughter." When Vicky left the house, she was happy. As she glanced back, her grandmother waved goodbye and said, "See you soon!" Cathy sobbed, and her heart broke as they drove away.

> *"The Lord is close to the brokenhearted*
> *and saves those who are crushed in spirit."*
> *Psalm 34:18 (NIV)*

At age ten, Vicky's life was pulled apart, dismantled, and rearranged within a few minutes. She left without her belongings, and her little shoes were still by the front door. Mark legally removed Vicky from her home, family, and friends, then transitioned her into an atheist home, where she was not allowed to mention God or her faith. She was forced to change schools and was no longer permitted to attend church activities, cheerleading events, or participate with her gym-nastics team. Life was very different — she was confused and sad. She missed her family.

Vicky was allowed to have a Bible in her new home, but her father made fun of God and openly mocked Him. Cathy shared, "When we were able to talk, I would remind Vicky that God loves her and is always with her. I would suggest she pray silently and remember what she learned in Sunday School and church."

> *"The Lord is a refuge for the oppressed,*
> *a stronghold in times of trouble." Psalm 9:9 (NIV)*

Cathy and her husband tried to fight the court's guardianship deci-sion but failed. They had no legal recourse because they willingly gave up their guardianship. The courts would not entertain granting custody back to Debbie because she was strung out on drugs. Cathy shared, "The first year without Vicky was horrible. I worried about her and felt guilty. When we talked on the phone, she would cry and ask to come home. Our family was ripped apart because we did not understand grandparent's rights."

She continued, "Regrettably, we gave our legal guardianship rights back to Debbie because we were blinded by hope and love for our daughter. We thought she was doing better — we wanted her to be better. I learned when addiction is involved — you must put your grandchildren first and keep them safe. I failed Vicky."

"God is our refuge and strength,
an ever-present help in trouble." Psalm 46:1 (NIV)

As the months passed, Mark allowed Cathy and Vicky to see each other occasionally. They were both grateful for the time they had together but saying goodbye was always hard. One day while talking on the phone, Vicky sobbed and said, "I want to come home, but Dad won't let me, and he won't let me see my Mommy — This is all Mommy's fault because she keeps taking drugs. I don't think I will ever get to move back home." Cathy was distressed as she listened to Vicky cry, realizing there was nothing she could do to comfort her.

"He gives strength to the weary
and increases the power of the weak."
Isaiah 40:29 (NIV)

As the next two years passed, Cathy's world became dark — she felt very alone and discouraged. Then one day, a stranger sat by her at a conference, and they began talking about life. Cathy began to open up about her daughter's addiction, "It's excruciating to watch my beautiful daughter continue to struggle with heroin. The drugs have tormented her body and mind. She is strung-out most of the time."

"The light shines in the darkness,
and the darkness has not overcome it."
John 1:5 (NIV)

She continued, "I need to figure out how to create a new life without my granddaughter Vicky. I'm stuck. I don't know how to piece my life back together." She paused, then said, "I have never felt so far away from God as I do now. I know it is wrong to blame God, but I'm very angry with Him. I've lost friends — they no longer want to hear about my problems, and my husband of 34-years filed for divorce.

My family collapsed. I am looking for enough strength today to continue moving forward."

> *"From the ends of the earth I call to you,*
> *I call as my heart grows faint;*
> *lead me to the rock that is higher than I."*
> *Psalm 61:2 (NIV)*

Her new acquaintance listened, then compassionately responded, "Sometimes our problems and heartaches seem insurmountable. If we are not careful, we can quickly lose our perspective and focus. Without God, problems can begin to dominate our thoughts, conversations, and actions allowing the adversary to sneak into our lives, creating a dark and hopeless world. Then, before long, we can accidentally push God to the sidelines as we try to handle our anger, grief, and heartbreaks all alone."

> *"You, Lord, keep my lamp burning;*
> *My God turns my darkness into light."*
> *Psalm 18:28 (NIV)*

Her friend continued, "But there is good news — You are never alone! When you feel overwhelmed or lost, "look up" for help and comfort. God will meet you right where you are! Embrace Him! His grace, unconditional love, and wisdom will sustain you as He carries you forward." She then gave Cathy some suggestions on different ways to embrace God to help her move forward.

> *"I lift up my eyes to the mountains—where does*
> *my help come from? My help comes from the Lord,*
> *the Maker of heaven and earth." Psalm 121:1-2 (NIV)*

Cathy listened and decided to take some baby steps with God. "I changed my daily prayer about Vicky. For the past three years, I begged God to bring Vicky home. I now pray for Mark and his wife to be good, loving parents, and to keep my granddaughter safe. By placing Vicky in God's hands versus carrying the burdens alone, my anger is going away, and my perspective on life is improving. I am grateful."

*"Trust in the Lord with all your heart and lean not
on your own understanding; in all your ways submit to him,
and he will make your paths straight." Proverbs 3:5-6 (NIV)*

"I now realize, God placed the stranger in my life, and I am grateful. I needed someone to help me place things into perspective. I'm finally able to see some positive things in my life, versus only darkness. I recognize that Mark loves his daughter, and this comforts me. Mark is allowing Vicky to visit more frequently, and she spends some weekends with me. I am grateful."

Cathy continued, "My divorce is almost final, but my husband did visit this past weekend. My brother will be moving in with me this spring, and we are planning to read the Bible together. I am reaching out to educate grandparents about their legal rights, and this chapter is an example of how I am sharing my story. I continue to pray that Debbie will overcome her addiction, but more importantly, I pray for God's will in her life."

*"The Lord is near to all who call on him,
to all who call on him in truth." Psalm 145:18 (NIV)*

"If you are raising grandchildren due to addiction, make sure you obtain legal guardianship, and never let go of your rights. With addiction, especially heroin, there can be devasting relapses. Addiction is a life-long disease — but there is hope, and His name is God!"

*"I have told you these things,
so that in me you may have peace.
In this world you will have trouble. But take heart!
I have overcome the world." John 16:33 (NIV)*

Author's Note: We sometimes face unexpected circumstances and heartaches that lack a clear ending. We endure ups and downs that feel like a rollercoaster, including sharp corners and gut-wrenching falls. However, there is good news! Regardless of our situation, God will sustain us as we open our hearts and invite Him into our storms. He will provide us with enough strength for today and hope for tomorrow. Simply believe in Him as you embrace His promises, and take another step forward.

REFLECTION

Addiction shatters the lives of people and families throughout the world. It knows no boundaries as it impacts rich and poor people, men, women, teens, children, brothers, sisters, mothers, fathers, aunts, uncles, cousins, and friends. However, there is good news! God restores broken lives and families.

1. Do you know someone or a family that has been impacted by addiction? If you answered yes, what happened? Are you praying for this person or family? Are you taking the time to listen and encourage them?

_____

_____

_____

_____

2. When you face problems in your life, are you seeking "God's will" for the situation? Are you asking Him for wisdom, courage, and comfort to move forward?

_____

_____

_____

_____

NEXT STEPS

1. Do you know a grandparent who is raising their grandchildren due to a family addiction? Perhaps an aunt or uncle who has stepped in to raise their niece or nephew due to addiction issues?
    If you answered yes, suggest they seek legal advice regarding formal guardianship/legal custody to ensure the courts protect the children.

2. There are resources and support groups to help addicts and the families of addicts. If you want or need to seek professional help for yourself or a loved one, below are some contacts and resources. Remember, you are not alone!

    *   SAMHSA National Helpline for Substance Abuse and Treatment 24/7 1-800-662-HELP (4357)
    *   Celebrate Recovery https://www.celebraterecovery.com
    *   Narcotics Anonymous https://www.na.org/
    *   Nar-Anon for Families and Friends of Addicts https://www.nar-anon.org/
    *   Alcoholics Anonymous® http://www.aa.org
    *   Al-Anon® for Families and Friends of Alcoholics https://al-anon.org
    *   Alateen® https://al-anon.org/for-members/group-resources/alateen/
    *   NOPE (Narcotics Overdose Prevention & Education http://www.nopetaskforce.org/
    *   Local Women Centers
    *   Homeless Shelters
    *   Employee Assistance Programs through your employer
    *   Your Pastor, Minister, or Priest
    *   Your doctor, local hospital, or community church can provide you with a list of counselors if you want or need help.
    *   Family Members or Friends

CLOSING PRAYER

If you, a loved one, or dear friend is struggling with addiction, pray this prayer below. God will be listening!

Dear Heavenly Father,

Today, I come to you with a heavy heart. I pray for _____, who is suffering from addiction. Please give (me/him/her) the strength, wisdom, and courage to seek help and break free from this horrible bondage and suffering. Help (me/him/her) to believe in your healing power and to accept the help of others. Please fill (my/his/her) heart and mind with your love, compassion, and strength. I praise you and thank you. Amen.

Life is Not Always Easy

"And the peace of God, which transcends all understanding,
will guard your hearts and your minds in Christ Jesus."
Philippians 4:7 (NIV)

Rachel opened her eyes from a deep sleep and began gasping for air. Her abusive, estranged husband was in her bedroom, quietly sitting on the edge of her bed, staring at her while she slept. She trembled and feared for her life.

Rachel's story began many years earlier. Growing up in the Midwest, she appeared to have a happy childhood, including a warm home, caring parents, and three brothers. Her mother was previously married, so her two older half-brothers lived in a different state. Rachel's family visited her older brothers once a year, which was very exciting. Life seemed normal. She had the opportunity to attend church every once in a while, just often enough to learn that God loved her. She understood God was with her and watched over her.

As the years moved on, she began to sense her family was suppressing a painful secret. At age twelve, Rachel accidentally discovered a giant shot of whiskey in their dishwasher. She was stunned as the truth slowly emerged — a situation that changed her life forever. Her mother was an alcoholic who drank from morning to night and would frequently pass out. Rachel's father was also an alcoholic, but he was able to hold a job. For some reason, Rachel had been blind to the reality in her own home. Unfortunately, the effects of alcohol eventually fractured her parent's marriage, and they divorced, leaving Rachel heartbroken and confused.

During her teenage years, Rachel did her best to attend school while dealing with her Mom's situation. She loved her Mom and empathized with her, but assuming the caregiver role for an alcoholic parent was extremely difficult. Embarrassment, stress, anxiety, exhaustion, and fear became part of her routine. Rachel would often say a quick prayer and ask God for strength. On the really tough days, she could feel God comforting her with an unexplainable sense of peace. She was grateful for her Heavenly Father and the courage He provided in the silence of her home.

> *"Peace I leave with you; my peace I give you.*
> *I do not give to you as the world gives.*
> *Do not let your hearts be troubled*
> *and do not be afraid." John 14:27 (NIV)*

After high school graduation, Rachel continued to care for her mother. During this time, she met a man who made her feel special, and they began to date. He was kind, attentive, and caring — the type of man she wanted in her life.

After eighteen months, they were married. Rachel was excited to begin living a "normal" life with her new husband. Unfortunately, right after they were married, his job required a temporary move across the country. The thought of moving and leaving her family made Rachel nervous, but she was committed to her marriage. For that reason, she packed up their belongings and relocated with him.

Shortly after their move, to her dismay, Rachel's new husband transformed into a controlling and possessive person. At first, he screamed and called her horrible names. But soon, both verbal and emotional abuse became routine. She never knew what would trigger his anger, so she "walked on eggshells" as she strived to avoid his angry outbursts and fits of rage. She was afraid.

Rachel found herself in an unfamiliar town, isolated from her family and friends, with a husband who quickly escalated his abuse. He would pull her hair and pin her against the wall while yelling directly into her face and making threats. He would throw things at her while screaming vulgar names and obscenities. Rachel was petrified of her husband. She suffered from emotional humiliation. One night, he locked her out of their home during one of his outbursts. It was scary and embarrassing. Her self-esteem and self-worth were disappearing, and she felt trapped.

Then one day, she received a call. Her mother was dying from the effects of alcohol; time was short, and she needed to come quickly. Despite the resistance from her husband, she made the bold decision to fly home, walking away from her job. Rachel was a broken woman, but she wanted to see her mother before she died.

Upon arriving home, her mother's condition seemed to improve almost immediately, for no apparent reason. Over the next few weeks, every time Rachel decided to return to her abusive husband, her mother's condition deteriorated, and she would cancel her travel plans. It was at this point, Rachel began to pray simple prayers for peace and understanding. As the days passed, she could literally feel God carrying her, and she was grateful.

"Cast all your anxiety on Him because he cares for you."
1 Peter 5:7 (NIV)

For another five weeks, her mother's fragile condition shifted on a daily basis. One day she would rally, and the next day, she would deteriorate. As Rachel bravely faced the reality of her mother's situation, she continued to endure verbal assaults on the phone from her uncaring husband. Despite the gravity of her circumstances, she continued to pray and trust God.

Then, a remarkable phenomenon began to unfold in Rachel's life. Her constant state of fear and anxiety was slowly replaced by an indescribable sense of calm and renewed strength. It was as if God was showing her, "I'm here. I've got you!" For the first time in months, Rachel felt safe. Through her mother's final days, God removed her from an intolerable situation so she could gain strength and clarity regarding her next steps. She was thankful.

"For I am the Lord your God who takes hold of your
right hand and says to you, Do not fear; I will help you."
Isaiah 41:13 (NIV)

A week after her mother passed away, Rachel flew home with a transformed sense of self-esteem and strength. While she dreaded being back with her husband, she was excited about her relationship with God, so she immediately found a church to attend — this gave her hope.

> *"I can do all this through Him who gives me strength."*
> *Philippians 4:13 (NIV)*

Rachel soon learned she was pregnant with their first child. When she asked her husband when they could return home so she could be close to her family, he angrily stated they were never going back home. This was her new way of life. She felt trapped but decided to look up and trust God with her entire life. While carrying her first baby, she surrendered her life to God and was baptized.

Rachel gave birth to a beautiful baby boy, and within three years, delivered a second healthy son. Her husband's abuse continued, but she was grateful he never harmed their children. Rachel gives God credit for keeping her children safe while carrying her through the torturous days, weeks, and years of marriage. For a total of fourteen years, she lived in constant terror of her husband.

> *"But the Lord is faithful, and he will strengthen you and*
> *protect you from the evil one." 2 Thessalonians 3:3 (NIV)*

Then one day, her husband turned his verbal abuse toward their children. It was at that point, she realized her unhealthy marriage must come to an end. While she knew God did not like divorce, she also understood her Heavenly Father did not want one of His daughters living in an abusive marriage. Her eyes were finally wide open.

After deep self-reflection and many hours of prayer, Rachel filed for divorce. She was thankful the boys were safe with her, but realized the months and years to follow would not be easy. She placed their lives and their future in God's hands.

*"Trust in the Lord with all your heart and lean not
on your own understanding; in all your ways submit to him,
and he will make your paths straight." Proverbs 3:5-6 (NIV)*

The months leading up to the final divorce were tough. Despite living in separate homes, Rachel's estranged husband continued to bully and frighten her whenever possible. On more than one occasion, he entered her home while she was sleeping. Rachel would wake-up in the middle of the night only to see him sitting on the edge of her bed staring at her — it was creepy, and she feared for her life. He threated to take the children away on a daily basis and attempted to disrupt every area of her life. It was a stressful time, but through it all, she held on to God's promises in the Bible and continued to focus on Him.

As the weeks passed, Rachel began attending a different church with her boys and joined the church choir. The church family embraced and supported them. She never felt judged or "not accepted" because she was going through a divorce. Joy and happiness slowly emerged in her life. She had HOPE! Shortly after their divorce, her ex-husband began dating a woman and remarried. The craziness gradually subsided, and she had a renewed sense of peace in her life. She was grateful and free!

*When Jesus spoke again to the people, he said,
"I am the light of the world. Whoever follows me
will never walk in darkness, but will have the light of life."
John 8:12 (NIV)*

While attending church, Rachel met a caring and loving man named Kevin, who was also in the choir. They shared common interests, and she learned he also endured a painful divorce. Their friendship grew into love, and they were married.

Kevin made a focused effort to spend time with her sons and become a father figure. "Friday family nights" became a fun routine, from pizza to movies to a variety of outings. For the first time, Rachel and her boys experienced a healthy family unit. She was thrilled, and her boys loved their new step-father.

Two years into their marriage, Kevin began to experience extreme mood swings and unexplained erratic behaviors. He had periods of severe depression, episodes of aggression, followed by phases of intense mania, which led to massive credit card "buying sprees." Rachel was afraid as she watched her husband slipping away day after day.

As she continued to pray for clarity and strength, Kevin was finally diagnosed with an extreme form of adult-onset bipolar disorder. They were surprised by the diagnosis, but thankful to have an explanation for his volatile mood swings. His doctors immediately began to balance several medications to manage his condition. Despite their efforts, Kevin lost his job due to his variable and unpredictable behaviors.

As the months passed, Rachel became overwhelmed. Her husband went through many jobs, and their accumulating medical expenses placed the family's finances in a tailspin. They were facing staggering credit card debts that Kevin accumulated during his manic phases. Rachel started to find weekend jobs so they could pay their rent. Despite their severe financial problems, she continued to trust God and faithfully tithed; She knew God would never abandon her or her family.

Matthew 6:33-34 (NIV)

But seek first his kingdom and his righteousness,
and all these things will be given to you as well.
Therefore, do not worry about tomorrow,
for tomorrow will worry about itself.
Each day has enough trouble of its own.

Kevin's mental state continued to deteriorate despite the doctors' efforts to balance his medications. His depression deepened as their financial situation became grim. Lacking hope, he threatened to commit suicide on numerous occasions. He was unable to grasp what was happening to his body; Kevin felt like a failure.

Rachel was terrified as she cared for her husband, while balancing two jobs and raising her sons. She found herself in a pattern of praying, crying, and praying again as she held on to God's promises. Then, on a particularly tough day, Rachel respectfully asked God, "why is all this happening."

"In him and through faith in him we may approach
God with freedom and confidence." Ephesians 3:12 (NIV)

From that day forward, Rachel began to notice how God provided exactly what they needed to pay their bills and still have nutritious meals on the table. Sales popped up for groceries and the essentials items they needed, while unplanned weekend jobs provided extra income. When Rachel felt overwhelmed, "the right answers" popped into her head. It was at this juncture she once again had clarity; God was guiding and providing for her family in the middle of their trials and tribulations. Rachel was not alone. God filled her with His peace and courage as she continued to move forward.

"So do not fear, for I am with you; Do not be dismayed,
for I am your God. I will strengthen you and help you;
I will uphold you with my righteous right hand." Isaiah 41:10 (NIV)

As the months continued to pass, Kevin's health and work situation began to stabilize. They were grateful. Their lives and family life started to normalize, and they began to socialize with friends once again.

One weekend, they decided to venture out and attend a Halloween party — they were excited. Rachel had a weekend job, so they drove in separate cars and met at the party. As the evening came to a close, she followed Kevin home.

At their designated exit, they drove down the off-ramp, then stopped at a traffic light. Suddenly, Rachel's car was violently struck from behind by a drunk driver traveling 80 mph. The impact thrust her car into Kevin's vehicle, leaving Rachel's car a heap of metal while his car sustained significant damage. Amazingly, thanks to God's grace, they both walked away from the crash site. Rachel, however, was plagued with on-going pain after the accident. She had a severe whiplash but later learned she also had Fibromyalgia.

Despite her new health challenges and financial pressures from the accident, Rachel pressed forward. Kevin's mood swings escalated again, and he lost additional jobs. While their finances were extremely tight, she knew many people had situations far worse; she was thankful for their blessings. Rachel did not have things she wanted, but God was faithfully providing the things they needed. She realized, material things are temporary, so she decided to build her treasures in heaven. This Bible passage comforted her regularly:

> ### *Matthew 6:25-27 (NIV)*
>
> Therefore, I tell you, do not worry about your life, what you will eat or drink; or about your body, what you will wear. Is not life more than food, and the body more than clothes?
>
> Look at the birds of the air; they do not sow or reap or store away in barns, and yet your heavenly Father feeds them. Are you not much more valuable than they?
>
> Can any one of you by worrying add a single hour to your life?

As time past, their oldest son Doug graduated from high school and pursued a successful vocational career. Their youngest son Mark was doing well in high school, but he was concerned about his friend who was living out of a car. Rachel wanted to help others and be God's hands and feet here on earth. They opened their home to this discouraged young man. For the next three years, he lived with them as a member of their extended family. Unfortunately, during this time, the boys began to experiment with drugs.

As life progressed, Doug was married, Mark graduated from high school, and the young man they accepted into their home moved on. Rachel received a small, unplanned inheritance, which helped ease some of their financial burdens. Just as things started to fall into place, their lives were turned upside down once again. There was no way to anticipate the painful struggles the family would face in the upcoming months.

Through a routine annual exam and mammogram, Rachel learned she had breast cancer. Tests also indicated she had precancer cells in her cervix. Devastated, Rachel leaned on her faith once again and quietly sang the chorus, "Because He Lives, I Can Face Tomorrow" over and over again. She proceeded with a double mastectomy and treatments for cervical pre-cancer. Thank God, no chemotherapy was required.

Then, Rachel received a terrifying phone call. Her oldest son Doug was burned in a home accident, leaving him in the hospital burn unit for several weeks. Rachel was petrified. She found herself on her knees once again, sobbing and begging for God's healing hands. Through prayer and faith, Doug pulled through. After multiple skin grafts, he was able to return to his job. Rachel praised God for healing Doug and the incredible strength he provided during this traumatic event.

In the midst of Rachel's health scare and Doug's accident, Mark's drug usage escalated, despite his continual denials and mood swings. He had run-ins with the law and landed in jail on two separate occasions. Then, one day, their home was robbed. Numerous items were taken, including special and sentimental things. Rachel was afraid and heartbroken at the thought of her son or one of his friends committing the robbery, but she realized it was a definite possibility.

The situation hit a boiling point when the police stormed into their home to search Mark's room. The police knew he was not only a heroin addict but also a drug dealer; they were watching him. Rachel was shocked and sobbed as the reality of the situation unfolded; she was terrified for her son and heartbroken. She thought to herself, "How can this be? What have we done wrong?" That night, she prayed harder than ever before, asking God to save her son. Her knees were weak, and she could hardly stand due to her broken heart.

"...and call on me in the day of trouble; I will deliver you,
and you will honor me." Psalm 50:15 (NIV)

When a second robbery occurred, Mark moved out of their home. It was heartbreaking as they watched him relocate into a run-down, dirty, local motel where other drug addicts lived. His girlfriend joined him, staying up many nights to ensure he did not overdose. Mark had no money for food, and his ribs showed through his clothes due to malnutrition. Rachel continued to pray for him and believed as long as he was breathing, there was hope he could be saved.

Despite their limited income, Rachel started taking dinner to Mark and his girlfriend. Going to the motel was scary, but she trusted God to keep her safe. Driving into the motel parking lot, night after night, broke her heart. Everywhere she looked, there were unsupervised, small children running around in the dark and cold, without jackets. Wanting to help in some small way, she began shopping at a local thrift store to purchase coats for the children. She would bring the coats home, lovingly wash and pray over them, then give them away. The children were excited to receive their gifts. It filled her heart with joy and peace as she reached out to others in need. She also realized that serving God through others helped take her mind off Mark's dire situation.

"Share with the Lord's people who are in need.
Practice hospitality." Romans 12:13 (NIV)

After months of drug dealing, turmoil, and unrest, Mark ended up in prison for nine months. Rachel was relieved to have Mark out of the drug-infested motel and away from his friends. She prayed for his safety and freedom from his drug addiction.

While Mark was in prison, Rachel learned that one of his childhood friends was living on the street in over 100-degree summer temperatures with a pregnant girlfriend. The young woman was five months pregnant and expecting twins. The situation broke Rachel's heart, and she thought, "What would Jesus do?" After many discussions and days of prayer, Kevin and Rachel took in the young couple until they found other accommodations for them. During this time,

God took care of their finances once again. They were grateful for the opportunity to help this couple and their unborn babies.

"And do not forget to do good and to share with others,
for with such sacrifices, God is pleased." Hebrews 13:16 (NIV)

When Mark was released from prison, he was no longer on drugs but was suffering from extreme delusions. It was unclear if the delusions and hallucinations were from his past drug use or if they stemmed from other health issues. He had no place to go and no income.

Kevin and Rachel decided to open their home once again and help their son rebuild his life. While his mood swings have decreased, they continue to seek professional support for his delusions, which can sometimes result in aggressive behavior and terrifying incidents. Rachel and Kevin are hopeful and committed to prayer for Mark's full recovery.

"Be joyful in hope, patient in affliction, faithful in prayer."
Romans 12:12 (NIV)

During their numerous personal storms, Rachel and Kevin were blessed to attend a church that focused on "being the hands and feet of God" in the local community. Today, they continue to support a variety of outreach programs to help the homeless, widows, divorced women, and hurting people. Rachel can feel her faith grow as she serves those in need, whether it be through the church or on her own. It fills her with joy and peace to help others. As she describes it, "It sustains me!"

In closing, Rachel cannot explain all the challenges in her life, but she knows God is with her family through every storm. The adversary seeks to attack and destroy. Thankfully, there is good news — God prevails! Rachel does her best to hold on to God's promises and peace while striving to look forward and not backward. She shared, "Always know that God is with you. He will guide you during your darkest hours. Our lives on earth are temporary — I look forward to eternal life in heaven!"

"...In this world, you will have trouble. But take heart!
I have overcome the world." John 16:33 (NIV)

REFLECTION

As we saw in Rachel's story, God "showed up" numerous times to help in various ways throughout her life. Pause and Reflect.

1. Have there been times when God helped you? If you answered yes, describe what happened?

_____

_____

_____

_____

_____

_____

_____

2. God is with us all the time and reveals Himself to us in many ways. How can you "take time" to notice and appreciate the small, big, and unexpected ways God helps you every day?'

_____

_____

_____

_____

_____

_____

_____

NEXT STEPS

Depending on your situation, there are a variety of resources available to help you as you move forward, including family, friends, support groups, and local churches. If you want or need to seek professional help, below are some additional resources. Remember, you are not alone.

- If you feel you are in immediate danger, call the police at 911
- National Domestic Violence Hotline 1-800-799-7233
- SAMHSA National Helpline for Substance Abuse and Mental Health 1-800-662-HELP (4357)
- Alcoholics Anonymous® http://www.aa.org
- Local Women Shelters
- Your local church or hospital can provide you with a list of counselors if you want or need help to overcome abuse or addictions, including alcohol, drugs, gambling, pornography, or other challenges you are facing.

CLOSING PRAYER

Dear God,

Thank you for the many blessings in my life. When times are tough, and I am in the middle of a personal storm, please help me to remember that you are with me. Thank you for your guidance, peace, and unconditional love. Amen.

Finding Joy After Heartbreak

"...Do not grieve, for the joy of the Lord is your strength."
Nehemiah 8:10 (NIV)

Mike was paralyzed, unable to move from the neck down. Within months, he lost his ability to speak. Trapped in his failing body, Mike discovered he could communicate through blinking. During the final days of his life, by the flickering of his eyes, he strived to share his love with family and friends.

Mike's journey began in a small town, nestled in the state of Wyoming. When he was born, his parents were best friends with a couple who had a baby girl named Sue. Mike and Sue would take their naps together, while their moms played afternoon bridge and supported each other through motherhood. Both families believed there was a God, but only occasionally attended church, and rarely prayed or read the Bible.

When Sue was in the fourth grade, her father accepted a job that required a move. Sadly, the families parted ways, intending to keep in touch and visit regularly. Unfortunately, distance and life separated the families; they lost touch, other than an occasional note or Christmas card.

When Mike graduated from high school, he began attending the University of Wyoming (UW). At the beginning of his sophomore year, his Mom received an unexpected note from her longtime friend, sharing that Sue was also attending UW. What a coincidence, or was it? Aware that Mike was looking for someone to date, his Mom suggested he reach out to Sue. Surprisingly, he followed her suggestion! Within months, Mike and Sue fell "madly in love." After a romantic courtship, they were married and moved into student housing. Sue quit school to support her new husband while he finished the ROTC program and graduated from the university.

Upon graduation, Mike was commissioned into the Army. Sue was pregnant when he received his first assignment. They picked up their belongings and moved to Georgia, followed by a second move to North Carolina. Before long, the Army sent Mike to Vietnam. While he was deployed, Sue returned to her hometown in Wyoming to raise their five-month-old son. She missed Mike terribly, but settled into a small apartment and began to make new friends.

Before long, Sue established a friendship with a woman named Grace, who lived in the same apartment complex. From their first meeting, Sue sensed there was something different about her new friend but could not explain it. Her friend seemed to radiate a special peace and joy that piqued Sue's interest. Sue later learned that Grace was praying for her; Prayers that would be answered in a few years.

As time passed, Mike remained in Vietnam. During his time there, he had the opportunity to hear a chaplain speak openly and honestly about God. The chaplain's words spoke directly to his heart and moved him. For the first time, he realized and believed that God was real! That day in Vietnam on Cam Rahn Bay changed his life forever. On the beach, outside a chapel, he fell facedown in the sand and prayed a simple prayer, "Lord, if you will protect me, my wife, and my son, I will serve you." Mike immediately felt different and transformed, but it was hard to explain.

> *"For God so loved the world that he gave*
> *his one and only Son, that whoever believes in him*
> *shall not perish but have eternal life." John 3:16 (NIV)*

Mike wrote a letter to Sue, indicating he had become a Christian. Sue was happy for him but did not understand what that meant. She was rather confused. When Mike was discharged from the Army and returned to Wyoming, they started looking for a church to attend. Sue did not grasp his desire to attend church but wanted to support her husband. During this time, they were blessed with a second son as Mike continued to search for a fulfilling job.

Finally, thanks to a connection from Sue's friend Grace, Mike landed a job in Denver, Colorado. They packed up their belongings, leaving their friends and family behind, and moved 300 miles away. Little did they know, Grace had arranged for some Christian friends in Denver to "watch over" Sue and her family.

As they settled into their new home, Sue was invited to attend a Christian's Women's Club with the wife of Mike's new boss. She was uncomfortable about the invitation but reluctantly participated in a few meetings to be respectful. Then, during one club meeting, an unexpected experience occurred as she intently listened to the speaker. Sue's heart was touched. For the first time, she believed the word of God, understood the plan for salvation, and embraced it. It was an unbelievable moment. Sue immediately felt joy and peace in her heart, and for the first time, grasped the transformation Mike experienced on the beach in Vietnam. Grace's prayers were answered.

> *"...Everyone who calls on the name of the Lord*
> *will be saved." Romans 10:13 (NIV)*

At last, Mike and Sue were on the same page! They found a church for their family to attend, and it felt like home. As their love for God grew, their respect and admiration for each other also multiplied. They were deeply in love.

Then one day, the church Pastor asked Mike and Sue if they would consider leading a Sunday School class for young married couples. They were thrilled and embraced the opportunity. Over time, their class participation grew to over 150 people. They found their passion and were grateful to serve the Lord as a team!

For the next fifteen years, life was calm, with only a few ups and downs — they were blessed and thankful. As their boys grew, Mike desired to start a business. Sue was nervous about this new venture but supported her husband's dream. Unfortunately, at the same time the company launched, the country slipped into a deep recession. The Denver economy took a significant hit. Mike's struggling business soon failed, and he found himself unemployed for the next year.

Despite their situation, they remained steadfast in their faith and prayed for a resolution to their current circumstances. They were grateful for Sue's salary but were forced to dip into their life savings to cover part of their monthly expenses. As a family, they were at peace and continued to trust God.

"Rejoice always, pray continually, give thanks
in all circumstances..." 1 Thessalonians 5:16-18 (NIV)

Their oldest son Brandon soon graduated from high school and was ready to attend college. While their finances were extremely tight, they saved just enough money to cover Brandon's first semester of college. They praised God when he received a full scholarship, and Mike was blessed with a new job opportunity in the Denver area. God was faithful once again!

"And my God will meet all your needs
according to the riches of his glory in Christ Jesus."
Philippians 4:19 (NIV)

The following year, Brandon was enjoying his sophomore year in college and training for a triathlon. He was at the peak of his training when he noticed a lump under his arm. His doctors decided to perform a biopsy, so Sue immediately headed to his university in California. To their shock, their oldest son had Stage 3 Hodgkin's Lymphoma. Brandon dropped out of college to undergo daily radiation treatments. Sue quit her job to care for him, as her family placed their faith in God for his complete recovery. During the long year of cancer treatments, Sue embraced the following Bible verse:

"You will keep in perfect peace those whose minds
are steadfast, because they trust in you."
Isaiah 26:3 (NIV)

Due to the massive radiation exposure, Brandon was informed he would never have children. Despite this heartbreaking news, he pressed forward while leaning on God and his family. He knew his Heavenly Father had a purpose for his life — to help others while giving them hope. As the year progressed, their church family and friends continued to bombard heaven with prayers for his complete healing. The Lord answered those prayers. Brandon returned to college the following year, cancer-free. Our Heavenly Father called him to become a doctor, so he faithfully changed his major and looked forward.

As time passed, Mike's career flourished, and he was offered a new job with expanded responsibilities. After many prayers, Mike, Sue, and their youngest son Cody relocated to Texas, just as Brandon finished college and entered medical school. They again found a great church and taught the young married Sunday School class. Life was full and exciting.

> *"May the God of hope fill you with all joy and peace*
> *as you trust in him, so that you may overflow with hope*
> *by the power of the Holy Spirit." Romans 15:13 (NIV)*

Several years later, Mike was offered a significant promotion and relocation opportunity. It was his dream job in Arlington, Virginia. The timing seemed right — Cody was now a police officer while Brandon was happily married, enjoying his career as a doctor, and still cancer-free. After many prayers, Sue and Mike embraced this opportunity and moved across the country. They were excited to explore the next chapter of their lives together.

While in Virginia, Mike served on the board of directors for their church, the USO for Washington DC, and other key industry associations. Sue and Mike continued to proactively mentor young married couples and openly share God's love with others. When time permitted, they hopped on their Harley to enjoy the beautiful backroads of Virginia and Maryland. Life was great, but an unexpected storm was beginning to brew in their lives.

Mike began to experience odd physical symptoms, including light-headedness, fainting, and urological problems. Then additional

issues surfaced, including coordination problems, walking challenges, and stiffness. As his symptoms continued to progress, it
became difficult to perform his demanding job.

Ultimately, Mike had no choice but to take an early retirement so
he could focus on "getting healthy." He fully intended to return to
work once his doctors resolved his health issues. With many things
up in the air, Sue and Mike felt it was time to be close to their
family, so they returned to the Denver area, as they continued to
pray for Mike's complete healing.

> *"...In this world you will have trouble.*
> *But take heart! I have overcome the world."*
> *John 16:33 (NIV)*

Unfortunately, Mike's health continued to deteriorate after their
move. After numerous doctors and a wide variety of medical tests,
he was finally diagnosed with a rare disease called Multiple System
Atrophy (MSA). The progressive, debilitating, neurological disease
had no known cure. The diagnosis was basically a "death sen-
tence" unless God performed a miracle. After hearing the shocking
news, Mike asked his doctor if anyone had survived MSA, and the
doctor bluntly stated, "No. None." Sue and Mike were stunned
but knew their Heavenly Father would carry them through this
unplanned journey. They prayed for a miracle if it was God's will
and the strength to persevere.

> *"So do not fear, for I am with you;*
> *do not be dismayed, for I am your God.*
> *I will strengthen you and help you;*
> *I will uphold you with my righteous right hand."*
> *Isaiah 41:10 (NIV)*

As time progressed, the effects of MSA took control of Mike's body.
Together, they mourned as they watched his independence slowly
deteriorate and slip away. His once determined walk became
staggered, first requiring canes and then a walker. The relentless
disease did not stop there. He soon transitioned to a powered
wheelchair and later became completely bedridden, reliant on Sue
and a power lift to move. Finally, Mike was paralyzed from the neck

down — his earthly body was failing. Despite the severity of their situation, together, they found peace, comfort, and joy through prayer and their reliance on God.

"My grace is sufficient for you, for my
power is made perfect in weakness."
2 Corinthians 12:9 (NIV)

Despite the horrific physical effects of his illness, Mike and Sue's faith in their Heavenly Father expanded as they continued to lean on Him for strength. God blessed them, both emotionally and spiritually, during this painful time. They spent many hours talking about heaven. Mike once told Sue, "I pray if I am not healed here on earth — I want to be a living testimony of God's love, his mercy, and grace." Grateful for their Heavenly Father's love and support, they decided to journal the final months of Mike's life so they could share their Lord's amazing grace with others.

"And if I go and prepare a place for you,
I will come back and take you to be with me
that you also may be where I am." John 14:3 (NIV)

Nine months before he passed away, Mike shared his views regarding the illness that was taking control of his body. As he spoke, Sue carefully recorded his words in their journal: "The proper perspective of a terminal illness for a believer reflects the end of a disease, not the person! When the disease dies, the person (believer) is healed and assumes a new body, without pain and suffering!" Mike fully embraced the promises of Jesus and was at peace for the journey he was facing. He knew if God did not perform a miracle on earth, he would be healed in heaven.

When Jesus spoke again to the people, he said,
"I am the light of the world. Whoever follows me will
never walk in darkness, but will have the light of life."
John 8:12 (NIV)

Mike embraced the opportunity to minister and pray for people, including the hospice caregivers who assisted Sue. He once shared, "When I worked, my purpose was to glorify our God in all that I did. I was to reflect peace, joy, love, and hope. Now, I can't move, but the purpose of my life is to honor God and allow him to use me in any way — to glorify him. I still have peace, joy, love, and hope. I thank the Lord for sustaining that."

"The fruit of the Spirit is love, joy, peace, patience, kindness,
goodness, faithfulness, gentleness, and self-control."
Galatians 5:22-23 (NIV)

When asked how he could sustain his sense of peace, Mike replied, "It's because I know as a certainty, when I die, I'm going to heaven."

Jesus said to her, "I am the resurrection and the life.
The one who believes in me will live, even though they die."
John 11:25 (NIV)

Mike was unable to speak the last six months of his life. Trapped in his failing body, he discovered he could communicate through blinking and eye movements. Sue shared, "During his final days, through the flickering of his eyes, he strived to share his love with family and friends. Then, one night, Mike went to sleep and woke up in heaven."

After forty-one amazing years of marriage, Sue was alone, without the love of her life. Their romance story ended. As Sue paused to reflect on the final journey with Mike, she shared, "God blessed me with a wonderful husband. It was a privilege and honor to care for him during his illness. I can still remember gently washing Mike's face as he would lovingly gaze into my eyes and thank me. I praise my Heavenly Father for providing me with the strength and peace to care for my husband during his long walk to heaven. When I felt overwhelmed and exhausted, I could feel God carrying me as if He was saying, 'I'm here. I'm with you!'"

"The Lord is my strength and my shield;
my heart trusts in him, and he helps me.
My heart leaps for joy, and with my song
I praise him." Psalm 28:7 (NIV)

In closing, Sue remarked, "I miss Mike every day and miss being married, but through the grace of God, I choose to live in joy. By trusting God and allowing Him to comfort me, I am able to comfort others as they grieve the loss of their loved ones. Our Heavenly Father gave me a new purpose — I support a Widows Group. I enjoy my mom, two sons, and four wonderful grandchildren. Brandon is cancer-free and was blessed with two healthy, miracle children several years after his radiation treatments! Life goes on with purpose and meaning as I enjoy my personal relationship with God!"

Psalm 68:4-5 (NIV)

Sing to God, sing in praise of his name,
extol him who rides on the clouds;
rejoice before him — his name is the Lord.
A father to the fatherless,
a defender of widows,
is God in his holy dwelling.

Mike and Sue

REFLECTION

As we saw in Mike and Sue's story, regardless of the events or circumstances in their lives, they continued to trust God.

Pause and Reflect.

1. Are you fully trusting God with your life?

_____

_____

_____

_____

2. Do you pray and ask God for guidance and direction? Do you pray daily, or only when you need His help?

_____

_____

_____

_____

NEXT STEPS

Living a life centered around God was the cornerstone of Mike and Sue's successful marriage. They embraced the "Fruit of the Spirit" (*love, joy, peace, patience, kindness, goodness, faithfulness, gentleness, and self-control*) even during their toughest days.

1. Pause and Reflect. Can you see or feel the "Fruit of the Spirit" in your daily life? If yes, please describe below:

_____

_____

_____

2. Are there some adjustments you want to make in your life with God's help? If yes, what do you want to adjust?

_____

_____

_____

_____

_____

3. Mike and Sue had a personal relationship with God. If you want a deeper relationship with God, turn to the last page of this book for a time of personal reflection.

_____

_____

_____

_____

_____

CLOSING PRAYER

Dear God,

Thank you for carrying me through my tough times. I am currently struggling with _____, and I need your help. Please give me the strength, peace, and wisdom I need to persevere. When I am afraid or frustrated, please comfort me. When I do not know what to do, please guide and direct me.

Thank you for your unconditional love. Amen.

A Non-Believer Finds God

*"Now faith is confidence in what we hope for
and assurance about what we do not see."*
Hebrews 11:1 (NIV)

Everything crashed and burned that horrific morning. But to Tony and Deborah's surprise, during their darkest moments, heartbreak, and anger, God showed up in miraculous ways! Through His grace and love, their broken family began to heal as their lives transformed forever.

Tony and Deborah first met on a softball field in Georgia, thanks to an introduction by her brother. Through their co-ed softball team, they quickly established a great friendship. They enjoyed each other's company.

Deborah was a single mother of two daughters, which was not easy. Her parents disowned her several years earlier — they did not approve of her lifestyle. Being estranged from her parents broke Deborah's heart, but she did her best to cope and move forward. Through all the ups and downs of the family, her daughters remained close to her parents.

Tony also had a rough relationship with his parents. He grew up in a home environment that lacked love and encouragement. His mother was very abusive while his father was passive. He felt like a burden in his own home versus a loved child. He sought refuge and enjoyment through his singing.

Tony joined the Navy after graduating from high school, to escape his home life. He shared, "The Navy raised me, so I decided to make it a career." He did not know much about religion and ignored it — considering himself to be "agnostic." Tony married at a young age and had two daughters, whom he loved very much. Unfortunately, his marriage fell apart. Seeing no hope for restoration, he filed for divorce.

Before long, Deborah and Tony's friendship on the softball field grew into love. Within months, they decided to get married. As they started their new life together, her daughters lived with them, and his daughters stayed with his ex-wife.

During their second year of marriage, Tony received transfer orders from the Navy, which required relocation to Hawaii. It was a significant change for both of Deborah's girls, but her youngest daughter Ashleigh, who was twelve years old, became rebellious due to the move. She resented leaving her home, friends, and grandparents. While in Hawaii, she started to run away, and eventually, she was "kicked out" of school. Ashleigh was out of control, and her parents did not know where to turn or what to do.

Luke 11:9-11 (NIV)

Ask, and it will be given to you;
seek and you will find;
knock and the door will be opened to you.

For everyone who asks receives;
the one who seeks finds;
and to the one who knocks,
the door will be opened.

The turmoil with Ashleigh was exhausting and placed enormous stress on their marriage. The constant friction finally hit a boiling point. One day, after a heated argument, Deborah packed-up the girls, left Tony in Hawaii, and moved back to Georgia. Tony loved Deborah and was able to obtain transfer orders back to Georgia, where they reconciled, and he retired.

To their dismay, the transition back to Georgia did not resolve the challenges with Ashleigh. It was just the beginning of many turbulent years. When Ashleigh turned fifteen, she was influenced by a friend to begin cutting and using cocaine. As her situation deteriorated, she lived with her grandparents and a friend for a while, but nothing seemed to help.

Ashleigh's unstable lifestyle persisted throughout her high school years. She managed to graduate, then moved in with her boyfriend while continuing her "party lifestyle." Before long, Ashleigh was pregnant with a cutting addiction; her arms were covered with scars. Then one day, when she was seven months pregnant, her boyfriend walked out.

Distraught and sobbing, Ashleigh called her mom at work, then stopped answering her phone. Fearing the worst, Deborah rushed to her daughter's apartment, but no one came to the door. She panicked, thinking Ashleigh severed a vein when she was cutting, placing both herself and unborn baby in jeopardy. Unsure where to turn, Deborah dialed 911.

Thankfully, Ashleigh finally answered the door when the police arrived, but she was emotionally unstable. Deborah had no choice but to have her daughter committed for a 72-hour psychiatric observation period. Ashleigh hated her mother for this action and did not allow Deborah to see her new granddaughter named Catie until she was two months old.

The non-stop roller coaster with Ashleigh continued despite the birth of her daughter. On one occasion, she slashed the tires of the car owned by her mother's boss, because she was angry. Ashleigh was arrested and placed on probation. Deborah was shocked and mortified by her daughter's actions.

"Consequently, whoever rebels against the authority
is rebelling against what God has instituted,
and those who do so will bring judgment on themselves."
Romans 13:2 (NIV)

During this time of upheaval, Deborah wanted to mend the estranged relationship with her mother and father, so she purchased some flowers and drove to her parent's home. She was not allowed in their house, but her mom came out and took the flowers. Deborah told her mother, "I love you, and I am sorry." Her mom never responded, turned around, and went back into the house. Deborah was sad but grateful she tried to make amends. Two months later, her mother became ill and passed away. At that time, she reunited with her father.

As life continued, so did the trials with Ashleigh's lifestyle. She started to see Catie's father again — so they could do drugs together. Then, one summer day, when he was babysitting little Catie, he left her alone in a hot car while shopping at Walmart. Catie was blood red and soaking wet when she was discovered.

Deborah knew she must take action to protect her granddaughter, so she made the difficult decision to call Family and Children's Services (FCS) to file a formal complaint. The courts reviewed the case and granted Tony and Deborah temporary guardianship of Catie. They immediately asked Ashleigh to move back home with them; their goal was to keep their granddaughter safe, not to separate Ashleigh from her daughter.

"God is our refuge and strength,
an ever-present help in trouble." Psalm 46:1 (NIV)

About six weeks later, the courts granted Ashleigh full custody of her daughter. Tony and Deborah were devastated when they moved out, realizing little Catie would once again be subjected to Ashleigh's party lifestyle. Fearing for the baby's safety, they reopened their home with an agreement Ashleigh could not refuse. Tony and Deborah would care for Catie and keep her safe, while their daughter partied whenever and however she wished.

"Cast your cares on the Lord,
and he will sustain you..." Psalm 55:22 (NIV)

As the years passed, Ashleigh started to settle down. She met a nice man, fell in love, and was married. Around this time, Tony and Deborah moved about forty-five minutes away to pursue new job opportunities. As a result of this move, Ashleigh and her husband rented her parent's vacant home. Unfortunately, due to various reasons, they failed to pay rent or utilities, and it placed a long-lasting financial burden on Deborah and Tony.

> *"...In this world you will have trouble. But take heart!*
> *I have overcome the world." John 16:33 (NIV)*

During the first year of Ashleigh's marriage, they had a friend who hit some rough times, so they invited him to move into their home. Before long, this man and Ashleigh had an affair. Her husband was devastated; he left and filed for divorce. To complicate the situation, she was pregnant with this man's baby, but he also walked out.

Now alone and pregnant, Ashleigh was responsible for her five-year-old daughter Catie while working and continuing to party. After many discussions, Tony and Deborah again opened their home to their daughter and granddaughter. They agreed to be tolerant of Ashleigh's lifestyle, doing their best to protect Catie and their future granddaughter. It was a great offer, so Ashleigh packed up her belongings and moved to South Carolina.

> *"Be strong in the Lord and in his mighty power."*
> *Ephesians 6:10 (NIV)*

Within a few months, Ashleigh went into labor, but there were some complications. When Beth was born, all her vitals were okay, but she did not cry or make any noise for about eight hours. It alarmed Deborah, but things appeared to be okay when the hospital released her.

Ashleigh finally settled down after Beth was born. Tony and Deborah were committed to "watch over" their daughter and grandchildren, keeping them safe in a loving home. Ashleigh enrolled little Beth in a nearby child daycare center while she worked, and Catie attended school. Life seemed to be "going pretty well," with the five of them living under one roof.

As the months began to pass, Beth grew and grew. She was a happy, healthy baby, and they all loved her; she brought "hope" into their home. They fondly remember one special March evening when they enjoyed holding Beth and watching Catie play, before following their regular bedtime routine. As the evening came to a close, they remember kissing the children goodnight and safely tucking them into their beds.

Deborah was an early riser and awoke at 3:30 the next morning. After getting ready for the day, she walked into the baby's room and slowly bent down to kiss her granddaughter's little face, but Beth was ice cold. As panic filled her body, Deborah flipped on the light switch, suddenly realizing Beth was blue and not breathing. Immediately, she started CPR and screamed for Ashleigh to get Tony, but Ashleigh could not move and kept yelling, "No. No. No."

CPR was not working, so Deborah started running through the house, screaming, "Dial 911, the baby's dead." As Tony rushed to little Beth's room, Deborah pleaded, "Get her to wake up. Get her to wake up." On his knees, Tony tried to revive her and pleaded with God to make her breathe. Then he briefly thought, "who am I to ask God for help." When the emergency technicians arrived, there was nothing they could do. Beth was only four months old when she passed away from Sudden Infant Death Syndrome (SIDS).

Tony shared, "Everything crashed and burned that morning. My whole philosophy concerning life, my thoughts about taking care of my family — everything changed. We were trying to do the right thing by taking care of our daughter and grandchildren. Beth passed away on my watch."

> *"The Lord is close to the brokenhearted*
> *and saves those who are crushed in spirit."*
> *Psalm 34:18 (NIV)*

They were extremely angry with God. Together, they screamed and cursed Him for taking their grandchild away. They were heartbroken and confused. Ashleigh was distraught. Tony shared, "Why would a loving God take the baby?" What they could not comprehend through their grief was the fact that God was with them and loved them unconditionally; a love they would watch unfold over the next days, weeks, months, and years.

> *"...And surely I am with you always,*
> *to the very end of the age." Matthew 28:20 (NIV)*

The days following Beth's death were a blur as they made funeral arrangements. Paralyzed in grief, they were astounded when Deborah's father "stepped in" to provide a cemetery plot, especially given the estranged relationship Deborah previously had with her parents. It was a powerful moment. Tony shared, "His heart was there for us."

Not sure what to do next, Tony went to Beth's daycare center to inform them of her death. It was his first time at the center, and he was surprised a church ran it. As he entered the building, he shared that Beth passed away, but was unprepared for their emotional reaction, and it "threw him." The workers, including the male center director, started to cry as they hugged him and each other. Their overwhelming and loving response was new to Tony since he grew up in a loveless home. He was shocked and amazed — their reaction and demeanor left a life-long impression.

Over the next days, people from the church started to show up at their door to drop-off food and offer their condolences. Tony, Deborah, and Ashleigh had never met any of these people; they were astounded with their generous outpouring of love. At this point, Tony started to think, "There are some amazing people in this world; some people sincerely care about others and don't want something in return. Maybe churches don't just want your money. Perhaps we are not here all by ourselves."

> *"Blessed are those who mourn,*
> *for they will be comforted." Matthew 5:4 (NIV)*

As the weeks passed, they returned to their jobs but continued to struggle with their anger and grief. On one particularly tough day, Tony closed the door to his office and sobbed. Then, he decided to write a letter to Beth, apologizing for not taking care of her. As Tony lovingly poured his heart, grief, and regrets onto a blank piece of paper, his healing journey began. Later that day, he shared the letter with Deborah, and they cried together. Through her tears, she asked Tony to turn his letter into a song so other people could hear his powerful message. He would later fulfill this request.

Around this time, one of Deborah's co-worker invited her to come to church, the same church that ran Beth's daycare center. She responded, "I don't know. Tony's not into religion." But, for some reason, Deborah extended the invitation, fully expecting his answer to be no. Surprisingly, Tony replied, "Yes, but I want to meet with the pastor first." So, a meeting was scheduled.

When they sat down to talk with the pastor, Tony's first question was, "Why did your God take the baby?" The Pastor paused for a brief moment, then thoughtfully and compassionately said, "I can't answer your question — all I can tell you is that you must trust God in everything that you do." Tony did not expect this straight-forward answer. Furthermore, the pastor had a remarkable sense of calm, and he was not trying to sell or push religion. Amazed, Tony said, "I want what you have, and I don't even understand it." They smiled and laughed together.

> *"Trust in the Lord with all your heart,*
> *and lean not on your own understanding."*
> Proverbs 3:5 (NIV)

Tony later shared, "The pastor's simple and honest statement probably had the biggest impact on my decision to try to figure out what God was all about." The next Sunday, Tony and Deborah attended church together. They cried through the entire church service, and it confused them. The songs touched their hearts, and the spoken words brought out incredible emotions. Intrigued, they went back to church the next Sunday and the next, fully expecting to hear they were going to hell — get out your wallets. But what they experienced was 180-degrees from their expectations — they were overwhelmed with hugging, love, and compassion from the people attending the church.

They loved riding motorcycles, and were invited to join a motor-cycle group at the church called "Driven by the Spirit." This group, especially the leader and his wife, embraced Tony and Deborah as part of their family, sharing God's love through their actions, encouragement, and prayers. It was a surprising journey, as they began to have fun while learning about God's love through conversations, reading the Bible, and attending Bible studies. Slowly, Deborah and Tony started to open their hearts to God's love and peace.

> *"Peace I leave with you; my peace I give you.*
> *I do not give to you as the world gives.*
> *Do not let your hearts be troubled*
> *and do not be afraid." John 14:27 (NIV)*

Deborah and Tony continued to be concerned about their daughter. She once again was entangled with partying, alcohol, and drugs. They regularly asked her to attend church, but Ashleigh was angry and wanted nothing to do with God. Then, one week, when they invited her, she said, "Maybe." However, she went partying on Saturday night and was still not home on Sunday morning when they left for church with their granddaughter Catie.

When they came home from church, Ashleigh was there. Deborah felt compelled to inquire about her unwillingness to attend church, her partying, and approach to life. They had a heated, verbal discussion. Then, Ashleigh yelled, "I don't believe in God. He wouldn't take a baby." Deborah responded, "If you don't believe in God, where do you think Beth is right now?"

Ashleigh began to sob and ran to the back of the house to escape the conversation. Deborah followed her, then lovingly said, "Beth is in heaven. I don't know about you, but I'm doing everything I can to get to heaven so I can see Beth again."

Ashleigh was in church the next Sunday. She still had a tremendous amount of anger, but she started reading the Bible and slowly began to open her heart to God. Then, one week, there was a revival at the church with a pastor they did not know. Ashleigh attended the second night with her mom and Tony.

At the end of the evening church service, the guest pastor asked people to make their way to the front of the church if they wanted or needed a "prayer of healing." Ashleigh grabbed Deborah's hand

and said, "I want to go." So, together, they went to the front of the church.

As they kneeled, the pastor prayed for each person. When he came to Deborah, the pastor said, "You had to be the strong one. You haven't been able to grieve". He then said to Ashleigh, "No mother should have to go through what you have gone through." Ashleigh sobbed as this stranger touched her heart. God knew what she needed to hear. She instantly believed and changed how she was living her life. From that point forward, Deborah and Ashleigh's relationship evolved into a loving mother and daughter relationship.

"He heals the brokenhearted
and binds up their wounds." Psalm 147:3 (NIV)

As the months passed, Deborah strived to expand her knowledge about God and the Bible before fully surrendering her life to Him. She attended Bible studies whenever possible, asked questions, listened, and prayed. During this time, she quit her job to take care of her father, who was extremely ill. Tony and Deborah were already under extreme financial hardships due to all their expenses related to Ashleigh and their previous home, but they wanted to do this for her father.

Jesus replied, "What is impossible with man
is possible with God." Luke 18:27 (NIV)

With the help of hospice, Deborah lovingly took care of her father. During this time, their relationship transformed; they experienced a wonderful season of healing and renewal. During her father's final days, Deborah received an amazing gift from God that impacted her life forever. As her father was dying, he opened his eyes and pointed up, then clearly said, "There's the baby." He then closed his eyes and never spoke again. Deborah knew he saw Beth as he was passing away. She shared, "The moment when my father saw Beth, changed who I am as a Christian today. I no longer questioned my faith. That is when I truly began to understand that God had a purpose for me."

> ### *John 14:2-3 (NIV)*
>
> My Father's house has many rooms;
> if that were not so, would I have told you that
> I am going there to prepare a place for you?
>
> And if I go and prepare a place for you,
> I will come back and take you to be with me
> that you also may be where I am.

A few months later, at a church retreat, as Deborah sat quietly in her cabin reading a devotional, the power of God's love surrounded her. She realized her anger was finally gone and replaced with the peace and calm of God. Everything changed in that life-altering moment, and she was grateful.

> *"You will keep in perfect peace*
> *those whose minds are steadfast,*
> *because they trust in you." Isaiah 26:3 (NIV)*

With a sense of urgency, she asked to be baptized to demonstrate she was "all in for God." So, on a cold twenty-degree morning, their pastor layered-up in warm clothing, walked down to the icy river, and baptized Deborah. Tony played his guitar and sang, as he watched from the shoreline. Deborah shared, "When our pastor dunked me, I closed my eyes. I never felt the cold water, just the warmth of God. A bright, white light surrounded me as a wonderful, peaceful feeling encircled me. It just felt right."

> *"For it is by grace you have been saved, through faith —*
> *and this is not from yourselves, it is the gift of God."*
> *Ephesians 2:8 (NIV)*

Tony shared, "Watching Deborah's baptism was very emotional, and, to be honest, I was a little envious as I continued to waiver with my personal beliefs. I kept trying to analyze every little aspect about God, and I would get confused. I would also think about the decades I had been disrespectful to God, and it bothered me."

*"If we confess our sins, he is faithful and just
and will forgive us our sins and purify us
from all unrighteousness." 1 John 1:9 (NIV)*

Tony continued, "Then, one day, I realized what it feels like to only trust humans — they regularly disappointed and failed me. But Jesus gave his life for me, for all of us so that we can have eternal life. My mind and heart were finally clear. I could no longer imagine life on this earth without loving the Lord. I decided to stop analyzing the things which confused me and trust God, just as the pastor recommended three years earlier." With that realization, Tony was also "all in," and was baptized.

*"Thanks be to God, who delivers me through
Jesus Christ, our Lord!" Romans 7:25 (NIV)*

Their decision to become Christians did not stop the challenges in their lives, but they no longer carried their heartbreaks and problems alone, thanks to their faith. God promises to be with us in our storms; He never promised that our lives would be conflict-free. As life unfolded, Tony lost his job.

They were already financially strapped due to their prior challenges with Ashleigh, compounded by the financial strain of Deborah quitting her job to care for her father. Tony and Deborah were grateful they could help their family, but now they were forced to deplete their retirement savings to pay their monthly bills. Deborah shared, "You have faith in God, even when things are tough." As their unemployment continued, they lost everything — but through it all, they were at peace. They knew God was with them, and He had a plan for their future.

*"For I know the plans I have for you," declares the Lord,
"plans to prosper you and not to harm you,
plans to give you hope and a future." Jeremiah 29:11 (NIV)*

After a year of unemployment, Tony received a job offer in California, but the position was placed on hold due to a hiring freeze. They kept trusting God and held on to their faith. After a few additional months, everything fell into place. They packed their truck with clothes, a guitar, a dog, their last $5000, and headed west. They strongly felt God called them to California to help Ashleigh begin living on her own and to support a church in a remote desert town.

In closing, Tony now has a great job with the government and leads the music ministry program at their church. Deborah manages the church office where they worship. Tony shared, "I never thought I would say this, but God blessed us when we lost our granddaughter. I know what life was like without God, and I now know the difference. We lost Beth, and we will never forget her, but we found peace because we are now walking with the Lord. I can't imagine ever going back and living life without God."

"...my hope, Lord, is in you."
Psalm 25:21 (NIV)

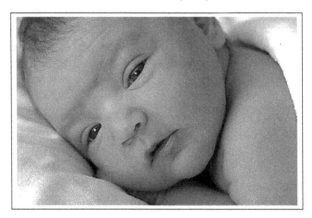

Beth

REFLECTION

As we saw in Tony and Deborah's story, when Beth passed away, God provided comfort "through people" they did not know. Strangers cried with them, brought food to their home, listened, and just loved them with no strings attached. Pause and Reflect.

1. Have you been "a stranger" who helped someone in need? How did you help?

   _____

   _____

   _____

   _____

2. What are some ways you can share God's unconditional love with hurting people?

   _____

   _____

   _____

   _____

3. Has God placed people in your life to carry you through a tough time? What happened?

   _____

   _____

   _____

   _____

NEXT STEPS

1. God provides wisdom, peace, and strength during the toughest times of our life. Circle all the areas below where you need His help and guidance today:

Job / Career	Finances	Anger	Weight Issues
Family	Unemployment	Worry	Depression
Marriage	Stress / Anxiety	Fear	Family Death
Children	Past Mistakes	Cheating	Trusting God
In-Laws	Self-Esteem	Addictions	Resentment
Health	Relationships	Letting Go	Infertility
Lack of Faith	Pride	Judging	Other Issues

Dear God,

You know my heart, my concerns, and my needs. Please give me the wisdom, strength, and peace to deal with the areas that I have circled above. Thank you for loving me unconditionally. Amen.

2. List some ways that you can strengthen your relationship with God today:

_____

_____

_____

_____

CLOSING PRAYER

Dear God,

Sometimes my journey on earth is heartbreaking, gut-wrenching, and confusing. Please help me to understand and comprehend that you are always with me — even when my human brain is unable to rationalize the events in my life. Thank you for never leaving me alone in this unpredictable world. My hope is in you Lord! Amen.

Growing Old with God

"Do not cast me away when I am old;
do not forsake me when my strength is gone."
Psalm 71:9 (NIV)

Barb was born into a modest, Christian home in 1928. She entered the world during the "Roaring Twenties" when Calvin Coolidge was president, and prohibition was the law of the land. Much has changed over the years, but one thing has remained steadfast and true, her relationship with God.

One late afternoon, while sipping a cup of tea, Barb reflected on the past ninety years of her life. "I've seen so much over the years. I remember going to school with my grandfather in a Model-T Ford, living through the devasting 1933 Long Beach earthquake, and standing in long lines with ration stamps during World War II. As I close my eyes, I can still see my Mom bartering for services with her homemade canned peaches and hear Kate Smith sing "God Bless America" for the first time on the radio. We chewed tar off the roads, since we could not afford chewing gum, and played with mercury, which is now considered to be a hazardous material. Oh my, how things have changed during the various seasons of my life."

"There is a time for everything, and a season
for every activity under the heavens." Ecclesiastes 3:1 (NIV)

As she continued to reflect, "When I was growing up, Sundays were always a day of worship for my family. We attended church, had family dinners with my aunts, cousins, and grandparents, then enjoyed singing church hymns as my mother played the piano. Life was simple, and our resources were limited, but we knew God loved us!"

"For you have been my hope, Sovereign Lord,
my confidence since my youth." Psalm 71:5 (NIV)

Barb paused to take another sip of tea, then continued, "Living through World War II by the Southern California coastline was very scary at night. Due to the war, we were required to keep our windows covered, so enemy planes could not see our homes near the Southern California shoreline. Each night, my mother and I prayed we would be safe."

"So, do not fear, for I am with you..."
Isaiah 41:10 (NIV)

"I can still remember one scary night when the air raid sirens sounded in the distance. My Dad was a War Warden for our neighborhood, so he quickly dressed in dark clothing, put on a special hat, then headed out to ensure our neighbors followed the blackout requirements. The smallest lights could result in an enemy bombing."

"As my Dad left the house that particular evening, my heart pounded. I was terrified. For some reason, I jumped out of bed, raised the blind covering the bedroom window, and gazed up at the night sky. I was shocked to see searchlights crisscrossing back and forth across the sky as the military searched for enemy planes. I panicked, ran back to bed, hid under my covers, and prayed— God, please keep us safe. I just wanted the sirens to stop."

"Be strong and courageous. Do not be afraid or
terrified because of them, for the Lord your God goes with you;
he will never leave you nor forsake you." Deuteronomy 31:6 (NIV)

When the war finally came to an end, church bells rang across the country in celebration. Barb shared, "When I heard the bells, I dropped what I was doing and ran to my church to join a prayer meeting of thanksgiving. We were so grateful the war was over, and God protected us."

"Therefore, I will praise you, Lord, among the nations;
I will sing the praises of your name." 2 Samuel 22:50 (NIV)

As Barb continued to talk, different events began to pop into her head. After graduating from high school, she started working for a loan company. At age nineteen, she was held up by a notorious bank robber, who was on the "FBI's Top 10 Most Wanted List." Barb shared, "Lloyd Sampsell, known as the Yacht Bandit, shoved a pistol in my back as he directed me to the bank safe early one morning. I was terrified. Later that year, Sampsell killed a person during another bank robbery."

"We can let traumatic events in our lives define us, or we can choose to place our trust in the Lord, seek His peace, and move forward with our lives. If we become paralyzed due to events in our lives and focus on the past, we can't accomplish the plans God has for us. Throughout my life, I have done my best to embrace a positive attitude, look up for strength, and trust God."

"Have I not commanded you? Be strong and courageous.
Do not be afraid; do not be discouraged, for the Lord your God
will be with you wherever you go." Joshua 1:9 (NIV)

Within a year of the robbery, Barb married a wonderful Christian man she met in high school and moved forward with her life. Then, in what seems like a blink of an eye, she enjoyed a career as an office manager, raised two daughters with her husband, and was blessed with three grandchildren. Barb shared, "Each year seemed to fly by faster and faster. When you are working full time and raising a family, life can be very busy and hectic. But through it all, my husband and I did our best to keep God first and show our family how to have a personal relationship with God."

As the years continued to rush by, Barb was suddenly in her sixties and entering the "retirement season of her life." She found herself balancing the joys of babysitting grandchildren with the heartbreaks associated with aging parents and in-laws. One by one, her parents and in-laws passed away while her husband's health deteriorated. Barb said, "During this difficult time, my faith in God deepened, and my dependence on our Lord expanded. He comforted me when my mother no longer knew who I was, and when my father took his last breath. God is always faithful."

When Barb turned seventy-four, her devoted husband passed away after fifty-three years of marriage. She was heartbroken, but once again leaned on her Heavenly Father for strength and peace. God was always with her, just as He promised. After a period of grieving, she made a conscious decision to remember the good times with her husband, embrace God's peace, and move forward with her life. She reminisces about her husband every day and wears his wedding ring close to her heart on a gold necklace. Barb is grateful for her memories.

"He heals the brokenhearted
and binds up their wounds." Psalm 147:3 (NIV)

Time continued to pass, and before long, Barb was celebrating her eightieth birthday. She paused to enjoy another sip of tea, then said, "When you're young, you think you have all the time in the world to enjoy life. Then, milestone birthdays begin to unfold, first forty and fifty, then before you know it, sixty, seventy, and eighty are at your doorstep. I've learned to be grateful for each new day and to not take things for granted. There are no guarantees we will be here tomorrow. We need to live our lives to the fullest and ensure our hearts align with God."

"...Let us rejoice today and be glad."
Psalm 118:24 (NIV)

"I also believe God gave me a mind, and it is my responsibility to keep it active. As times have changed, I've strived to stay current with technology as a way to remain connected with people. I learned to text, send emails, and use Facebook — a big change from listening to the radio when I was growing up. I try to remain creative by making gift baskets for my church and non-profit organizations. To keep my mind engaged, I watch Jeopardy nearly every night, and attend a weekly Bible study to expand my knowledge of the Bible."

She continued, "When I turned ninety, I thought, WOW — ninety is really old! But I know it's just a number, and I'm grateful to be alive. I'm still young at heart, but my human body is showing its age. My face appears to be growing new wrinkles (HA!), I walk with a cane, and getting up and down requires some extra effort. My memory has faded a bit, and I tire quickly, so I have learned to pace myself. I finally stopped dying my hair and let my gray shine through, but I did add a few highlights to keep things interesting. I love the following Bible verse regarding aging."

"Gray hair is a crown of splendor..."
Proverbs 16:31 (NIV)

"Despite some of my physical changes, I do my best to show God's love through my actions. I still bake over 150 dozen chocolate chip cookies to give away each year. I encourage the youth in our community through a smile, encouraging words, and raising funds for scholarships. By sponsoring a seeing-eye dog each year, I know I am helping someone less fortunate than me. Through my Sunday School class, I enjoy reaching out to college students by sending encouraging cards, small gifts, and of course, prayers. As an older member of our church, I have the opportunity to pray for people from my home and encourage others through phone calls. I want to continue to contribute."

"Throughout my life, I've enjoyed an on-going conversation with God. I don't use fancy words; I simply talk with Him like a daughter conversing with her Father. When I wake up in the morning, I always thank God for another day. I look forward to spending time with Him through prayer and reading the Bible. I openly share my praises, requests, hurts, and faults with Him. I am grateful He forgives and comforts me, as I continue my journey through life."

"Devote yourselves to prayer, being watchful and thankful."
Colossians 4:2 (NIV)

"I've embraced God's promises throughout my life, but as I've grown older, my faith and dependence on Him have expanded exponentially. I realize death will inevitably come to my doorstep, as it will for all of us, but I don't fear my future. I am grateful for the gift of eternal life that is available through Jesus."

"For God so loved the world, that he gave his only begotten Son,
that whosoever believeth in him should not perish,
but have everlasting life." John 3:16 (KJV)

In closing, Barb shared, "As people age, they still have many things to contribute. Remember to include older people and not discount their value. Cherish each day, and make sure you treasure the gift of life. Don't get discouraged — keep moving forward and looking up! God has you in the palm of His hand!"

Barb – Just before her 90th Birthday

REFLECTION

Growing old is part of life. Thankfully, God promises to be with us during all our seasons of life — including the good and tough times. Pause and reflect on the different seasons in your life.

1. Take a moment and jot down five of the happiest times in your life, then thank God.

_____

_____

_____

_____

_____

_____

_____

2. List some specific times when God carried you through an issue or problem, then pause and thank God for helping you.

_____

_____

_____

_____

_____

_____

_____

_____

NEXT STEPS

Below are some ways that you can follow God throughout the seasons of your life:

- Love one another. John 13:34
- Rejoice always, pray continually, give thanks in all circumstances. 1 Thessalonians 5:16-18
- Look to the Lord and His strength. Psalm 105:4
- Love your enemies. Luke 6:35
- Forgive people when they sin against you. Matthew 6:14
- Defend the rights of the poor and needy. Proverbs 31:9
- Trust in the Lord with all your heart. Proverbs 3:5
- Accept Jesus as your savior. John 3:16

CLOSING PRAYER

Dear Heavenly Father,

Thank you for my life, and the time I have here on earth. Please help me to fulfill your purpose for my life. Amen.

"For I know the plans I have for you," declares the Lord,
"plans to prosper you and not to harm you,
plans to give you hope and a future." Jeremiah 29:11 (NIV)

A Final Reflection

*"Trust in the Lord with all your heart and lean not on
your own understanding; in all your ways submit to him,
and he will make your paths straight."*
Proverbs 3:5-6 (NIV)

Life is a journey. As we have seen in the stories, there will be
highs and lows, twists and turns, and the inevitable blind curves
throughout our lives. No one ever said life would be easy. But
there is good news — we are not alone! God is with us! He will
carry us through our storms and tough times! He will never leave
us! Praise God!

Three Steps to Salvation

If you are interested in real victory –
a personal relationship with God,
follow the steps below.

1. Get Ready...

Admit you have sinned. Tell God what you have done, be sorry for it, and be willing to quit.

"For all have sinned and fall short of the glory of God."
Romans 3:23 (NIV)

2. Get Set...

Believe God loves you and sent His Son, Jesus, to save you from your sins. Accept the forgiveness God offers you.

"For God so loved the world that he gave his one
and only Son, that whoever believes in Him shall
not perish, but have eternal life." John 3:16 (NIV)

3. Go!

Claim Jesus as your Savior. Acknowledge God's forgiveness, respond with love, and follow Jesus.

"Everyone who calls on the name of the Lord
will be saved." Romans 10:13 (NIV)

Share your victory with a friend as you begin your new journey.

CPSIA information can be obtained
at www.ICGtesting.com
Printed in the USA
FSHW022323110220

9 781630 501662